The Origin and Principles of the American Revolution, Compared with the Origin and Principles of the French Revolution

Friedrich Gentz

The Origin and Principles of the American Revolution, Compared with the Origin and Principles of the French Revolution

FRIEDRICH GENTZ

Translated by
John Quincy Adams

Edited and with an Introduction by
Peter Koslowski

Liberty Fund, Inc.

Introduction, editorial additions, and index © 2010 by Liberty Fund, Inc.
Frontispiece from Wikimedia Commons

19   20   21   22   23   P   7   6   5   4   3

Library of Congress Cataloging-in-Publication Data

Gentz, Friedrich von, 1764–1832.
   [Ursprung und die Grundsätze der Amerikanischen Revolution, verglichen mit dem Ursprunge und den Grundsätzen der Französischen. English.]
   The origin and principles of the American Revolution, compared with the origin and principles of the French Revolution/Friedrich Gentz; translated by John Quincy Adams; edited and with an introduction by Peter Koslowski.
        p.   cm.
   "Translation of Der Ursprung und die Grundsätze der Amerikanischen Revolution, verglichen mit dem Ursprung und den Grundsätzen der Französischen. Reprinted with minor corrections from the 1800 edition published by A. Dickens, Philadelphia"—T.p. verso.
   Includes bibliographical references and index.
   ISBN 978-0-86597-820-1 (pbk.: alk. paper)
   1. United States—Politics and government—1775–1783.
2. France—Politics and government—1789–1799.
I. Adams, John Quincy, 1767–1848.   II. Title.
E211.G33 2010
973.3—dc22   2010013294

Liberty Fund, Inc.
11301 North Meridian Street
Carmel, Indiana 46032

Contents

Introduction

by Peter Koslowski

There may be no other two historical events that are of greater impact than the American and the French revolutions. The first gave birth to a new nation that was to develop into the leading power in the world a century and a half later. The second gave birth within a generation to the greatest power in Europe for about twenty years, changing all its neighbor states forever.

Friedrich Gentz (after being ennobled, Friedrich von Gentz) was born on 2 May 1764 at Breslau, Silesia (then Prussia, to-day Wroclaw, Poland), and died on 9 June 1832 at Weinhaus, near Vienna, Austria. Gentz's mother belonged to a Huguenot family that had fled France for Prussia and was related to the Prussian minister Friedrich Ancillon. Gentz spoke English and French very well, a fact that eased his career as a diplomat. His letters to the British Foreign Office are written in elegant French, the diplomatic language of Gentz's time.

The editor's notes follow the text. See p. 95.

Napoleon, the heir of the French Revolution, set out to rule all Europe until he was defeated by an alliance of all the major powers of Europe.

It is, however, not only power but ideas that changed as the result of the two revolutions and their revolutionary ideas. "The Ideas of 1776," of the American Revolution and of American independence, shaped Western constitutionalism and representative democracy; "the Ideas of 1789," the ideas of the French Revolution, led to a new civil law of the continental European states, to a new understanding of government and the relationships of state and church, and to realization of democratic government based on the concept of popular sovereignty. The French Revolution also gave birth to the spirit of revolution, to the idea that a nation can change itself by a total overthrow of its past and inherited character into an entirely new social body. This spirit of revolution has influenced all radical revolutions since then, especially the Russian Revolution of 1917. A comparison of the French and American revolutions is not only a study of world history, a study of the hour of the births of the American and the French Republic; it is also a study of the birth of the ideas that shaped all Western nations and all countries of the world searching for a constitution of liberty and democracy.

Friedrich Gentz is one of the first observers of both revolutions. Most of his continental contemporaries concentrated their attention on the French Revolution, which lay closer and had revolutionized the leading European countries. The United States of America was literally on the other side of the world from Europe. Those who had immigrated to America from Europe usually did not have the means to return. Gentz was prescient about the importance of the United States in its infancy, whereas his compatriots still looked at the United States as a half-civilized, distant land of little importance, considering Europe and the world to be shaped, as Leopold Ranke later put it, by the five Great Powers: Austria, Britain, France, Germany, and Russia. It is a paradox that the nation that sent the greatest number of people to the United States of America knew the least of all Western European nations about the United States. The German inability to grasp the potential of the United States, to which Gentz is the notable exception, had consequences well into the centuries. In both world wars, the German governments had no adequate perception of the economic and military power of the United States, yet Gentz was predicting this over a century earlier.

Although becoming more powerful in the eighteenth century, Britain was a maritime power, being at the same time inside and outside of Europe. France, not Britain, was the first continental power in the perception of Europeans. France had ended the Holy Roman Empire and had defeated Austria again and again. Gentz wrote about the subsidies paid to the Holy Roman Emperor by Britain. Finally, Napoleon divided Germany, just as Prussia, Russia, and Austria had divided Poland, remarking that he did to the Germans only what they had done to the Poles, although Russia got the largest share of Poland. Gentz

brought all his powers of argument and persuasion
to bear against Napoleon's attempt to legitimize the
expansion of the French Revolution. Gentz conceded
that the partition of Poland of 1792 was unjust, as was
every partition of any European nation. Although he
had been born in Prussia, he also believed that even
the Germans' self-partition into Prussia and Austria
was wrong, that it had been furthered by the French
Revolution's attempt to break away Prussia and other
German states from the old Holy Roman Empire. With
Edmund Burke, Gentz agreed that European nations
had no right to divide a European nation.

At the end of the eighteenth century, Britain was
looked upon with suspicion on the Continent. Britain's
colonial expansion seemed to contradict the doctrine
of the balance of power. In Europe, the British continued to insist on this balance of power, even though in
the greater world there was no balance of power any
more. Britannia ruled the waves, and she did nothing
to restore the balance of power except by driving the
North American colonies into rebellion.

Gentz was one of the few intellectuals who defended
Great Britain, arguing that it had become great by superiority in trade and industry and not by doing evil. It
was not Britain's and America's machinations, but their
commercial courage and genius that had given them
their economic superiority over the Continent, Gentz
wrote. The European nations are free to imitate Britain
in that, and all European nations could and should do
so. However, Gentz found hard to reconcile with free

trade the British Navigation Act, which permitted only British ships to transport goods to Britain. America, he was aware, was following Britain in trade and industry. Gentz received a lot of criticism for his defense of Britain and America; he was even called an Anglomaniac. The British Foreign Office paid him a generous monthly allowance for his reports to London.

Gentz was, however, never a British agent. When he was working for Prince Metternich later, the Austrian foreign minister and driving force at the Vienna Congress in 1815, Gentz insisted to the British that Metternich needed to be able to read all of Gentz's reports to and correspondence with the British government.

Gentz recognized that the founding of the French Republic in 1792 had led to escalating warfare, culminating in 1795 when the French army conquered the Netherlands and founded the Batavian Republic, trying to turn the proud trade power into a department of France. After the radical Directory had seized the supreme power in September 1795, external warfare increased even further when the revolutionary army attacked Germany, Austria, and Italy and marched on Vienna and Milan in 1796. The French Revolution continued the expansion that King Louis XIV had started. France had made large conquests in the Spanish Netherlands (Belgium) and in German lands on the left bank of the Rhine, particularly in Habsburg Alsace. But Louis XIV had not succeeded in realizing his ambition to extend France's eastern border all along the left bank of the Rhine, as the French Revolutionary War succeeded in doing in 1796. The French Revolution brought back to France the power and expansionism that the ancien régime of the monarchy had lost, particularly during the Seven Years' War of 1756 to 1763, known as the French and Indian War in North America.

Winston Churchill called this the first world war, a war fought not in one part of the world but in both hemispheres. It was fought between the European powers over territorial gains in the colonies and over predominance in Europe.

France's support for the American Revolution in the aftermath of this war between 1763 and 1788 produced mixed results for France herself, even though it helped to bring about the separation of the colonies from the British motherland. In spite of securing American independence, France was unable to extract considerable material gains from the American War of Independence. Rather the costs of fighting damaged the French national finances and contributed to the coming of the French Revolution.

Gentz writes at the end of his essay that he had set himself the goal of investigating the two world revolutions according to four principal points of view, "with regard to the lawfulness of the origin, character of conduct, quality of the object, and compass of resistance." (p. 93)

Can we judge unique historical events, such as these great revolutions, on the basis of general principles? *Revolution* is a generic term. Revolutions follow a scheme of actions of the same type. To revolutionize is to follow a pattern of action and to respond at the same time to the particular historical situation. Like any actions, revolutions must be judged by the circumstances preceding their beginning, by their origin. They must be judged by the character and quality in which they are conducted and carried through, by the conduct of the revolutionaries. They must further be judged by the quality of their goals, that is, by the revolutionary intention, and they must finally be judged by the extent of resistance or support they receive from the nation. In every action, the goal or intention is the beginning, and the realization of the goal is the consummation of the action. An action must be judged by the circumstances that set it in motion, by origin. It must further be judged by how the action is conducted, and finally by its success or failure. Revolutions are, of course, not only intentional actions but also events in which the acting persons are often driven by dynamics outside of their control. But revolutions are also political actions that can be judged as such. Gentz intended to judge the two revolutions as political actions and as historical events.

The North American colonies found themselves in an odd position when the conflict with Britain started, both inside and outside their motherland. They were required to pay taxes, but they had no voice in how those taxes were used. They were subjects of the British crown, yet had no seats in the British Parliament. They had to accept a British monopoly in trade with the colonies but could not export their own products to Britain.

Gentz points out the paradox of an American tax revenue to be paid for use only in Britain. This resembles the inconsistency of restricting the North American colonies to buying only British wares. Gentz compares Britain's trade monopoly in the colonies to a tax levied on North America, and he quotes the Second Continental Congress of the United States, which called the monopoly "the heaviest of all contributions." Gentz emphasizes the link between the impulse toward political control over a colony and the impulse to market control, limiting access to the market only to the motherland. It is inherent to being a colony that the motherland has a monopoly of trade and that the colony wishes to change this situation. Gentz clearly perceives the limits to the legitimacy of the colonial relationship: "The relation between a colony and the mother country is one of those, which will not bear a strong elucidation." (p. 19) The American Revolution brought to an end a strained and, from a natural-right point of view, an awkward relationship. Since there was little explicit legal definition of the relationship between the colonies and the motherland, the American Revolution did not have to break many laws. The colonies just applied to themselves such constitutional principles as parliamentary representation, which the motherland had applied to itself only.

The French Revolution acted within an elaborate, valid system of law under a king who was willing to enact constitutional reform. The revolution broke the law and killed the king. The French breach of law was far more extensive and serious than the colonial breach of law. In the end, the two revolutions are judged according to which broke more "real right." It is a breach of real right if one counters resistance to political action by violence that is out of proportion to that resistance. Violence must be minimized in political action. The French Revolution (and to an even greater extent the Russian Revolution) required an enormous degree of violence, with many victims. (It is an interesting question whether the National Socialist movement in Nazi Germany was a revolutionary movement, in this sense.) If a revolution needs to kill so many people to overcome the population's resistance, then by these lights, it cannot be legitimate, since its means are out of proportion with its goals. Gentz's criteria for judging eighteenth-century revolutions are even more applicable to the revolutions of the twentieth century.

The latest revolutions of our time, in the Czech Republic and East Germany in 1989, two hundred years after the French Revolution, have been called the Velvet Revolution and the Peaceful Revolution, respectively. Were they revolutions? Some have claimed that they were not true revolutions but rather implosions of two states of the former Warsaw Pact. Rosenstock-Huessy called revolutions like that semirevolutions (*Halbrevolutionen*).[1]

Gentz is a conservative and classical liberal. Like other conservatives, he does not like revolutions and does not believe in them, since he is convinced that the social world requires continuity and tradition. Conservatives also abhor the use of political violence for radical social change. In the end, Gentz comes to the conclusion that the American Revolution was a legitimate revolution, since it was not really a revolution. Its goal was to establish a constitutional regime that was in accordance with the British tradition of constitutional principles. The American Revolution did not unleash large-scale violence. It had clearly defined and limited goals. It finished revolutionalizing when these goals were reached. In general it succeeded in maintaining civilized conduct during its political fighting and military warfare. It did not aim at enforcing its principles on other nations.

All this cannot be said, according to Gentz, about the French Revolution: It used enormous violence. It faced very great internal resistance, which was overcome only by ruthless repression. (The people of Paris used to say that Robespierre was trying to reduce the population of the French Republic to one-half its pre-revolutionary numbers.) The goals or objectives of the French Revolution became more and more extensive and changed unpredictably under the varying influence of the different revolutionary factions. The French Revolution did not maintain good conduct. It did not come to an end by itself but was ended only by the ascent of Napoleon. Finally, it did try to enforce its principles on other nations.

Gentz is not only critical of the origins and historical conduct but also of the pivotal political ideas of the French Revolution. He considers the declaration of natural and unalienable rights of man as well as the idea of popular sovereignty to be superfluous rhetoric in the American Revolution and a dangerous illusion in the French Revolution. Although the French Revolution took over these two ideas from the American Revolution, through Jefferson's advice to Lafayette, these concepts were effective only in the French Revolution, according to Gentz, producing tremendous philosophical error, political disaster, and human misery.

The so-called rights of man are erroneous, Gentz believes, if they are used as an abstract claim against the concrete and real right. There is no right of man outside of the real right of the state. The French Revolution was an assault on the "real right" of states in the name of abstract and fictive revolutionary principles. If the French Republic absolved the subjects of the European states of their duty of obedience to their lawful governments, it created, according to Gentz, a situation like that during the religious wars, when various sides claimed to have the divine right to absolve their believers of their duty of obedience as citizens or subjects.

There is also no abstract sovereignty of the people, because the law is above any sovereign except God, and even God must be thought of as following the right He has set in place. The people or the nation cannot therefore simply call into being a law based on what it wills at any given time, as the French revolutionaries tried to do. The American Revolution and, following from it, the Constitution of the United States also follow the idea of popular sovereignty, but the right is constituted by the people, who are also bound by it. Both the people and the people's government are under the law. Gentz points out that this apparently small difference in the understanding of popular sovereignty is in fact no small difference at all. This is Gentz's central insight and also is arguably the greatest legacy of the American Revolution and the most important lesson to learn from the suffering of the French people in theirs.

The Origin and Principles of the American Revolution, Compared with the Origin and Principles of the French Revolution

Preface

The Essay, of which a translation is here given, was published in the *Historic Journal,* a monthly print which appears at Berlin; and was written by Mr. GENTZ, one of the most distinguished political writers in Germany. It is for two reasons highly interesting to Americans: First, because it contains the clearest account of the rise and progress of the revolution which established their independence, that has ever appeared within so small a compass; and secondly, because it rescues that revolution from the disgraceful imputation of having proceeded from the same principles as that of France. This error has no where been more frequently repeated, no where of more pernicious tendency than in America itself. It has been, here not simply a commonplace argument, as Mr. Gentz represents it to have been in Europe, but has been sanctioned by the authority of men, revered for their talents, and who at least ought to have known better.[1]

The essential difference between these two great events, in their *rise,* their *progress,* and their *termination,* is here shewn in various lights, one of which alone is sufficient for an honest man. A modern philosopher may contend that the sheriff, who executes a criminal, and the highwayman, who murders a traveller, act upon the same principles; the plain sense of mankind will still see the same difference between them, that is here proved between the American and French Revolutions.—The difference between *right* and *wrong*.

We presume it will afford a pure and honest gratification to the mind of every truly patriotic American reader,[2] to see the honourable testimony borne by an ingenious, well-informed, and impartial foreigner to the principles and conduct of our country's revolution. The judgment of a native American will naturally be biassed by those partialities in favour of his country, from which it is so difficult for the citizen to divest himself as an historian. The causes of hatred and affection must be more remote from the mind of a foreigner, and his decisions must therefore have a greater intrinsic value. The historian of his own country must always in some sort be considered as its advocate; but an impartial foreigner is its judge.

The approbation of such a writer as Mr. Gentz is the more precious too, for not being unqualified. The mild censure, which he passes upon certain parts of our proceedings is the strongest proof of his real impartiality; and though our sentiments as Americans may differ from his, upon various points of political speculation, we shall find very few, if any instances, that have incurred his censure, which our own candour will not equally disapprove.

Origin and Principles, &c.

The Revolution of North America, had, in the course of events, been the nearest neighbour to that of France.[1] A very considerable part of those, who were cotemporaries and witnesses of the latter had likewise survived the former. Some of the most important personages, who made a figure in the French revolution, scarce ten years before, had been active on the theatre of that in America.[2] The example of this undertaking, crowned with the most complete success, must have had a more immediate and powerful influence upon those, who destroyed the old government of France, than the example of any earlier European revolution: the circumstances, in which France was, at the breaking out of her revolution, had been, if not wholly, yet

In the following text, an asterisk indicates an author's footnote; arabic numbers indicate an editor's end note.

for the greatest part brought on by the part she had taken in that of America. In the conduct and language of most of the founders of the French revolution, it was impossible not to perceive an endeavour to imitate the course, the plans, the measures, the forms, and, in part, the language of those, who had conducted that of America; and to consider this, upon all occasions, as at once the model, and the justification of their own.

From all these causes, but especially because the recollection of the American revolution was yet fresh in every mind; because the principles to which it had given currency still sounded in every ear; because the preparatory temper of mind, which it had every where in Europe excited and left behind, favoured every similar, or only seemingly similar undertaking, it became so easy for those, who felt an evident interest in seeing the French revolution superficially compared, and thereby placed on the same ground, and confounded with that of America, to draw the great majority of the public into this fundamentally false point of view. At the period of great commotions, and of animated, vehement, widely grasping discussions, a very small number of men are able, and, perhaps, a still smaller number willing, with vigorous native energy, to penetrate into the essence of events, and take upon themselves the painful task of forming a judgment founded upon long meditation and persevering study. The similarity of the two revolutions was taken upon trust, and as many persons of respectable understanding and discernment had loudly and decisively declared themselves in favour of the American, it became a sort of accredited common-place, "that what had been just in America, could not be unjust in Europe."[3] As, further, the last result of the American revolution had been in the highest degree splendid and glorious; as its issue had been undoubtedly advantageous for America, undoubtedly advantageous for most other states, was undoubtedly advantageous for England herself; as this most important circumstance, and the greater moderation and impartiality which time and tranquillity always bring to the judgments of men, had at last reconciled with this revolution its most violent opponents; an irresistable analogy seemed to justify a similar expectation in respect to that of France; and a second common-place, far more dangerous than the first, because it seized its materials, in the empty space of distant futurity, gathered a great portion of the human race under the spell of the delusive hope, that "what in America, had conduced to the public benefit, will, and must, sooner or later, in France and throughout Europe conduce in like manner to the public benefit."

The melancholy experience of ten disasterous years,[4] has indeed considerably cooled down this belief; but it is not yet altogether extinguished; and even those who, have begun to totter in the faith, without, however, renouncing the principles, by which they justify the French revolution, extricate themselves from their perplexity, by recurring to external and accidental circumstances, which have hindered all the good that might have ensued, to the pretence that the revolution is not yet wholly completed, and to other equally nugatory subterfuges. The justice of the origin of both revolutions, they suppose to be taken for granted; and if one of them has produced more salutary consequences than the other, they impute this to Fortune, which here favours, and there abandons the undertakings of men.[5] An equality of wisdom in the founders of the two revolutions, upon the whole, is as much taken for granted, as an equality of integrity.

Hence, it will certainly be no ungrateful task to compare the two revolutions in their essential features, in their originating causes, and in their first principles with each other. But in order to prepare the way for such a comparison, it will not be superfluous to exhibit in a small compass, the principal features of the origin of the American revolution. It may justly be taken for granted, that since the last ten years have almost exhausted all the powers of attention and of memory, the characteristic features of the origin and first progress of that revolution are no longer distinctly present in the minds even of many of its cotemporaries: there are, besides, some points in the picture of this great event, which, at the time when it happened, escaped almost every observer; and which, not until a later period, discovered themselves in all their vivid colours to the piercing eyes of meditation and experience.*

The English colonies in North-America, far from being a designed regular institution of European wisdom, calculated for futurity, had been much more the pure production of European short-sightedness and injustice. Political and religious intolerance, political and religious convulsions, had driven the first settlers from their country: the single favour indulged them was to leave them to themselves. That their establishments were, in less than two hundred years, to form a great nation,[6] and to give the world a new form, was concealed no less to their own eyes, than to the eyes of those who had ejected them from their bosom.

In the apparent insignificance of those settlements, and in the false measure, by which the profound ignorance of the Europeans estimated the value of such distant possessions, lay the first ground of the extraordinary progress which the North American colonies had already made under the second and third generations of their new inhabitants. Gold and silver alone

---

* Thus, for example, among all the statesmen and literati, who spoke or wrote, either for or against the American revolution, there were only two, who even then foresaw that the loss of the colonies would be no misfortune to England: The one, Adam Smith, was at that time little read, and, perhaps, little understood: The other, Dean Tucker, was held an eccentric visionary.

could then attract the attention of European governments. A distant land, where neither of these was to be found, was, without hesitation, abandoned to its fortunes. From such a country was expected no *revenue;* and what increases not immediately the revenues of the state, could make no pretensions to its support, or to its particular care.

Nevertheless, by the peculiar, creative energy of a rapidly growing mass of enterprising and indefatigably active men, favoured by an extensive, fruitful, and happily situated territory; by simple forms of government, well adapted to their ends, and by profound peace, these colonies, thus neglected, and well nigh forgotten by the mother country, sprang up, after a short infancy, with giant strides, to the fulness and consistency of a brilliant youth. The phenomenon of their unexpected greatness, roused the Europeans, with sudden violence, from the slumber of a thoughtless indifference, and, at length, displayed to them a real new world, fully prepared to rivalize with the old; for which, however, at the same time, it was an inexhaustible source of wealth and enjoyment. Even before the middle of this century, every maritime power of Europe, but England more than all the rest, because the foundation of her colonies had accidentally departed the least from good principles, had discovered, that the peculiar, and only worth of all external European possessions, consisted in the extended market they opened to the industry of the mother country; that it was not the empty sovereignty over enormous territories; not the barren right of property to gold and silver mines; but solely the encreased facility of sale for European productions, and an advantageous exchange of them for the productions of the most distant regions, which gave to the discovery of America the first rank among all the events beneficial to the world.[7]

No sooner had this great truth begun to be so much as obscurely perceived, than necessarily all the exertions of the mother country concentrated themselves, in giving to their trade with the colonies the greatest extent, and the most advantageous direction; and for this end, even in times so little remote from the present, as those of which I speak, no other means were devised, than a *Monopoly*. In compelling the inhabitants of the colonies to receive exclusively from the mother country, all the necessary European articles they required, and to sell exclusively to her all the productions, by the circulation of which the merchants of the mother country might hope a certain profit, it was supposed that vast market, whose importance became more evident from year to year, would be improved in its whole extent, and under the most profitable conditions.

The error, which lay at the bottom of this system was pardonable. The genuine principles of the nature and sources of wealth, and of the true interests of commercial nations had scarcely yet germed in a few distinguished heads, and were not even developed, much less acknowledged. Nay, if at that early period, a single state could have soared to the elevation of these principles; on one side; had renounced all prejudices, on

the other, every paltry jealousy, and felt a lively conviction, that liberty and general competition must be
the basis of all true commercial policy, and the wisest
principle of trade with the colonies, yet could she not,
without sacrificing herself, have listened to this principle. For in leaving her colonies free, she would have
run the risque of seeing them fall into the hands of
another, who would exclude her from their market.
She was not privileged to be wise alone, and to have
expected a general concert among the commercial
powers would have been folly. As therefore a colonial
trade, grounded upon monopoly, was yet better than
none, there remained for a state, in the situation of
England, even had she most fortunately anticipated
the result of a long experience, and of profound meditation, no other system than that of *monopoly*.

To secure to herself the exclusive trade of the colonies was under these circumstances necessarily the
highest aim of England's policy. The establishment of
this exclusive trade, which naturally arose from the
original relations between the colonies and the mother
country, had not been difficult to the state; for the em-
igrants had never received the smallest support. By so
much the more expensive had it been to keep them.
The possession of the colonies was the occasion of
wars. The war of eight years between France and England, which concluded in the year 1763, by the peace
of Fontainebleau,[8] and which encreased the English
national debt nearly an hundred millions sterling, had
the colonial interest for its sole object. The conquest
of Canada would not in itself have been worth a tenth

part of the sums, which that war cost; the firm establishment of the commercial monopoly was properly
the final purpose, for which they were expended.[9]

It is a great question, whether even independent
of the unhappy differences, which broke out immediately after the close of that war, its consequences
would not have been rather pernicious than salutary
to England. The annihilation of the French power in
North-America completed the political existence of
the English colonies, and supported by the still ac-
celerating progress of their wealth, and of their vigor,
gave them a consciousness of security and of stability,
which must have become sooner or later dangerous to
their connection with the mother country. It is more
than improbable that this connection would have been
perpetual. It is difficult to believe that under the most
favourable circumstances it would have lasted another
century. No nation governed its colonies upon more
liberal and equitable principles than England; but
the unnatural system, which chained the growth of
a great people to the exclusive commercial interest
of a country, distant from them a thousand leagues,
even with the most liberal organization of which it was
capable, could not have lasted forever.* Yet it would

---

* So long as the colonists had found a paramount advantage
in the *culture of the land,* they would probably have borne their
dependence. But when the critical period had arrived, when
in the natural progress of society, a considerable part of the
capitals would have been employed in *manufactures,* the English monopoly would have become insupportable.

certainly have maintained itself for the next fifty years, and might perhaps have been dissolved in a milder and happier way than has now happened, had not England, under the most wretched of fascinations, fallen upon the idea of procuring in addition to the benefit of an exclusive trade, another immediate benefit, by an American public revenue.[10]

It is hard to decide, which of the secret motives, which on either side were imputed to the ministry of that time first gave existence to this pernicious project. The most pardonable of all, the wish of alleviating the burthen of taxes upon the people of Great Britain, and especially upon the land-holders; a burthen, which the war had so much aggravated, is unluckily at the same time the most improbable. Specie[11] was exactly that in which North America least abounded; to have levied in that country a tax of any real importance could scarcely have occurred to any Englishman with the least smattering of information; and that, amidst the thousand obstacles which must necessarily have opposed the collection of such a tax, its nett produce for the treasury would always have melted to nothing, could scarcely escape the sagacity of any person versed in the subject. If we consider it attentively on all sides; if we carefully remark certain expressions of the ministers of that day, and what were afterwards known to be their favourite ideas, as well as the whole course of transactions upon American affairs, we can hardly avoid the belief, that what is generally considered as the *consequence* of the first treasury plan, the jealousy of the parliament's unlimited supremacy was rather the proper motive for this plan; and the secret apprehension that America might grow weary of her fetters, misled them to the dangerous experiment of fastening still narrower chains upon her.

The first step in this untrodden career was taken immediately after the peace of 1763, and under the most unfavourable auspices. The minister of finance, George Grenville,[12] else in every respect an estimable and excellent statesman, but whose mind was either not great or not flexible enough to consider the new system in all its points of view, thought he could force down its execution, just at the period when, by various severe acts of parliament, he had brought back the commercial relations between England and the colonies as close as possible to the principles of monopoly; had pursued the American contraband trade, with the most oppressive regulations, and thereby had excited a great discontent in all minds. The tax with which he proposed to make his first essay, was a stamp-tax upon judicial records, newspapers, &c. to which the parliament, at the commencement of the year 1765, gave its assent.

The colonies had hitherto paid no other taxes, than those, which were necessary for the internal administration; and these proportionably insignificant charges had been prescribed and assessed by the several representative assemblies of each colony. In cases of urgency, for instance, in the course of the late war, these assemblies had raised, and presented to the government, extraordinary and voluntary contributions; but of a public tax, raised by act of parliament, there had been in North America no example. If the parliament, in the laws regulating trade, had sometimes introduced a trifling entrance, or clearance duty, the most distant trace had never appeared in any public transaction, of a design to make America contribute immediately to the general exigencies of the British empire.

A long and venerable *observance* had sanctioned this colonial immunity;[13] a thousand equitable considerations, and this above all, that the British commercial monopoly was of itself equivalent to a heavy and invaluable tax, justified this observance; and what was most important of all, even the authority of the parliament to violate this immunity, was controvertible with weapons furnished by the spirit of the English constitution itself. It had always been a favourite maxim of this constitution, that no Briton could be compelled to pay taxes, not imposed by his own representatives, and upon this maxim rested the whole constitutional power of the lower house in parliament. That the inhabitants of the colonies, in every sense of the word, were Britons, no man questioned; and the parliament, which thought itself authorised to tax them, even in that, recognized them as fellow citizens. Yet had they no representatives in parliament, and, owing to their distance, could properly make no pretensions to it. If, therefore, in respect to them, the constitutional principle retained its force, their contributions could only be prescribed by their colonial assemblies, and the British parliament was no more entitled to exercise the right of taxation over them, than over the people of Ireland.

But had this right been only questionable, it was at all events a false and hazardous step to bring it into discussion. To raise a controversy, concerning the bounds of the supreme power in the state, without the most urgent necessity, is in every case contrary to the simplest rules of state policy. Doubly dangerous must such a controversy here be, where it concerned a constitution, whose nature and boundaries had never yet been defined, and were, perhaps, not susceptible of definition. The relation between a colony and the mother country is one of those, which will not bear a strong elucidation; rights of sovereignty, of so peculiar and extraordinary a nature often vanish under the hands of those, who would dissect them. Now, when the mother country has a constitution like that of Britain, it becomes infinitely difficult to introduce into that relation a harmony, which satisfies the understanding, and at the same time the idea of right. It had never been examined how far the legislative authority of parliament, in respect to the colonies, extended; thus much, however, the colonies admitted, and would have continued long to admit, that the parliament was fully authorised to direct and to restrain their trade, in the widest extent of the word. This alone was clear; but this alone was essential to England. An attempt to go further was manifestly to set all at stake.

The appearance of the stamp-act in America was the signal for an universal commotion. The new laws against contraband trade had already irritated the minds of the people, because they plainly manifested the purpose of maintaining the British commercial monopoly in its greatest vigour; but these laws were received in silence, because there was no pretention to the right of complaining against them. Now, a new, and hitherto unexampled system, that of raising in North-America a tax for the treasury of England, was to be introduced, and in a form necessarily odious to the colonies; for a stamp-tax, from various local causes, had always been in North-America an oppressive tax. The opposition spread in a few days among all classes of people; in the lower, it burst forth in excesses of every kind; in the higher, by a stubborn and deliberate resistance, especially by a general agreement to import no merchandize from Great-Britain, until the stamp-act should be repealed. With the temper, which prevailed from one end of the colonies to the other, and with the well known perseverance, bordering upon obstinacy, of the author of the project, perhaps this first struggle might have ended in the total separation, had not just at that time the administration in England fallen into other hands.

The ministry, which in the summer of 1765, took the affairs of the nation in hand, rejected the new system of immediate taxation in America entirely. The mild principles, and the popular maxims of the marquis of Rockingham,[14] made him averse to a path, in which violence alone could lead to the goal; and the secretary of state, general Conway, had been, when the business was first transacted in parliament, Grenville's most powerful and ardent opposer. The stamp-act, in the first session of the year 1766, was repealed; but to preserve the honour of parliament from sinking altogether, with this repeal was connected a declaratory act, intituled, "An Act for securing the Dependence of the Colonies;" in which the right of Great-Britain to legislate for the colonies in all cases whatsoever, was solemnly maintained.

This last step could not, in itself, be indifferent to the Americans; yet the joy at the repeal of the stamp-act was so great, that no regard was paid to the possible consequences of the act, which was attached as a counterbalancing weight to this appeal; and probably peace and concord would have been for a long time restored and secured, had not the English ministry, in a luckless hour, brought again to light the fatal project of raising a revenue from America. The marquis of Rockingham's administration had been dissolved, soon after the repeal of the stamp-act, and had been succeeded by another, at the head of which was indeed the name, but no longer the genius of the earl of Chatham.[15] Charles Townsend, chancellor of the exchequer, a man of splendid talents, but of a frivolous and unsafe character, who was aiming to attain the highest summit of influence in the state, when an early death snatched him away from the career, proposed, in the year 1767, a tax upon the importation of glass, paper, painters' colours and tea into the colonies, and this proposal, although several of the ministers, and among the rest the duke of Grafton, who was at the head of the treasury department had silently contended against it, was by parliament adopted as a law. The defenders of this new plan entrenched themselves behind the feeble argument, that although parliament, by repealing the stamp-act, had renounced a direct taxation of the colonies, yet no renunciation could thence be inferred of indirect taxation, which was intimately connected with the right of regulating trade.

Had this reasoning even silenced the opposition in parliament, it was by no means calculated to satisfy the colonies. The hostile object of the new statute could not escape the shortest sight. The taxes prescribed, being announced merely as impost duties, were indeed reconcileable with the letter of that immunity, which lays so near the heart of the colonists, but their secret object could scarcely be any other, than to wrest by artifice, what was not ventured to be maintained by force. The insignificance of the benefit England could derive from these taxes, which would have produced only about £. 20,000, but too strongly confirmed this suspicion; and the peculiar character of the new regulations, the iniquity of exacting from a people, compelled to receive all the articles they needed, exclusively from the mother country, a tax upon the importation of such articles, rendered the undertaking completely odious. The imposts of 1767 operated in exactly the same manner as the stamp-act; the general non-importation agreement was renewed in all the colonies; bitter controversies between the colonial assemblies and the royal governors, violent scenes between the citizens of divers towns and the military, resistance on the one part, menaces on the other foreboded the stroke, which was soon to shake the British empire to its foundations.

The ministry seemed however to make one more stand, upon the very border of the precipice. In the year 1769, by a circular letter of the minister for the colonies, the pleasing prospect of a speedy relief from the odious impost duties was opened to the colonial assemblies, and the decided aversion of the duke of Grafton to the taxation of America, seemed to encourage the hopes which this letter had raised. But no sooner had he, in the beginning of 1770, resigned his office, than the affair took another turn. His successor, lord North,[16] did indeed in the first days of his administration formally propose the repeal of the American imposts, but with the unfortunate exception, that the tax upon tea should be continued as a proof of the legitimate authority of parliament; nor could the most vehement opposition of the united Rockingham and Grenville parties, who painted in the strongest colours the folly of continuing the contest, after the benefit was abandoned, avail any thing against this wretched plan.* From that hour it was clear that the ministry

* Lord North formally declared in parliament, that after what had happened, an entire repeal of all the new taxes could not take place, until America should be brought to the feet of Great-Britain.

had no other object than to make the colonies feel their chains. The first steps in this slippery career had their grounds in false representations and partial judgments; instead of these *errors* dangerous *passions* were now introduced, and the peace and welfare of the nation were to be sacrificed to a mistaken ambition, and a destructive jealousy.

Meanwhile, the disposition to resistance had struck deep roots in all the colonies; and the wider the mother country's undertakings departed from their first object, the more the resistance of the Americans departed from its original character. They had at first only denied the right of parliament to tax them; by degrees, the sphere of their opposition extended, and they began to call in question the authority of parliament altogether. When they had once taken this ground, it was in vain to hope to drive them from it. The consciousness of their stability, and their distance from England, their lawful pride in the rights, derived from their British descent, the recollection of the circumstances which had led their forefathers to America, the sight of the flourishing state into which in a period of 150 years they had turned an uninhabitable desert, the injustice, and the harshness of those, who instead of alleviating their dependence by gentle treatment, were daily seeking to render it more oppressive;—all this encouraged the new impulse, which their ideas and their wishes had taken. The folly of Great-Britain in abandoning, for the useless discussion of a problematic right, the undisturbed enjoyment of a connection, which though never analysed and dissected with theoretic accuracy, was even in its undefined state so advantageous, became continually more visible; but far from endeavouring with tender caution to heal the dangerous wound, measure upon measure was taken to inflame it. Almost every step taken by the government during this unhappy period, in respect to the internal administration of the colonies, to the courts of justice, to the provincial assemblies, to the relations between the civil and military authorities, seemed expressly calculated at once to embitter and to embolden discontent; and the spirit of insurrection had long been in full possession of every mind, when a new attempt of the ministry, made it suddenly burst forth with the utmost violence.

The persevering refusal of the Americans to import tea into the colonies, so long as the tax upon it, prescribed in the year 1767, and purposely retained in 1770, should not be repealed, had occasioned a considerable loss to the East-India company,[17] in whose magazines, great quantities of this article perished unconsumed. They had offered the minister to pay upon the exportation double the trifling tax of three pence upon the pound, which was yet so odious to the colonies; but this proposal, advantageous as it was, and which opened so honourable an issue from the crisis, was disapproved and rejected, as not according with the system of reducing America to unconditional submission. But as the embarrassment of the company was continually growing greater, they sought to help themselves by another project, and concluded to ship the tea for America upon their own account, there to pay the impost by their own agents and then make their sales. As at the same time, by act of parliament, the exportation was made duty free, whereby the tea, notwithstanding the impost in America, would be at a cheaper market than it had before been, it was hoped that the Americans would abandon all their scruples, and not feeling immediately the tax lurking in the price of the article, would give up all resistance.

The event soon discovered how vain this hope had been. Time had been allowed the colonies to reflect upon their situation, and to judge of the ministerial proceeding in the point of view which was alone essential. The merchants, who during the American agreement against the importation of British tea, had enriched themselves by the contraband trade of foreign teas, might, perhaps, only from mercantile considerations, abhor the undertaking of the East India company, sanctioned by the government; but the great mass of the people, and the most enlightend patriots in America, saw and condemned, in this undertaking, nothing but the evident purpose of carrying through the taxing right of the British parliament. The remarkable circumstance, that England had refused the larger revenue, which the taxes upon exportation from the British ports would have produced, to secure the levying of the much smaller entrance duty in America, betrayed a bitter passionate obstinacy, which together with so many other symptoms of hostility threatened the colonies with a gloomy futurity.

When the first report of these tea-ships having been sent arrived in America, from Newhampshire to Georgia, universal preparations for the most animated resistance were made. The agents of the company no where dared to receive the goods; in New-York, Philadelphia, and many other towns, such strong protestations against unlading the ships were made, that they were compelled to return untouched. In Boston, where the spirit of resistance had been from the beginning the most violent, Governor Hutchinson adopted measures to make the return of the ships impossible before the object should be attained; but his rigor only served to increase the evil. A small number of decided opponents, went on board the ship, and, without doing any other damage, broke open 342 chests of tea, and threw it into the sea.

The account of these tumultuous proceedings, soon after the opening of parliament, in the year 1774, reached England, where, immediately, the thirst for revenge silenced every other feeling; the zeal to maintain the honour and the rights of government, every other council, not only in the minds of the ministers, but likewise in the general opinion of the nation. In this critical moment it was forgotten, that it was not until after the colonies for ten years long, had been driven by a series of vicious and hazardous measures, by attacks continually repeated, and by studied systematic vexations to the utmost extremity, that their just indignation had burst forth in illegal acts.

The necessity for severe measures was indeed now evident, even to the moderate. But unfortunately, resentment overstepped the bounds of equity, and provoked pride the bounds of policy. The immediate authors of the excesses in Boston, might justly have been punished; the East-India company might justly claim to be indemnified by the colonies; the Americans, by their acts of violence, had evidently placed themselves at a disadvantage; and their faults gave the most favourable opportunity to bring them, with wisdom, back within their bounds. But England seemed herself to spurn all the advantages of her present situation, and to have commenced a war, rather against her own welfare and security, than against the opposition in the colonies. The first measure, proposed by lord North, was a law, to close as long as the king should think necessary, the port of Boston, and to transfer the customhouse of that flourishing and important commercial town to another place. Immediately after, appeared a second law, which struck still deeper at the vital principle of the colonies, which scarcely could be justified by the most exaggerated ideas of the parliament's authority, and which could not but unavoidably drive to despair, men, who had already been almost impelled to insurrection by an impost tax. This harsh law declared the province of Massachusetts Bay's charter void, and subjected this province, which by its wealth, its constitution hitherto, and the sentiments of its inhabitants, seemed to be more dangerous to the government, than all the rest, to a new organization, grounded on an absolute dependence upon the crown. At the same time, another act of parliament ordained, that persons, who during the tumults in America, had committed offences against public officers, in every case, where the governor should have reason to apprehend that they could have no impartial trial there, should be sent to England for trial; a statute, which according to British ideas, deserved the epithet of tyrannical. Finally, the minister brought into parliament a law, giving to the province of Canada, which had been until then under a merely temporary administration, a constitution entirely different from the forms of the other colonial governments; and however the most recent experience might seem to justify the government in this step, it could not but produce the most unfavourable operation in the colonies, who believed to read their own future destiny in the treatment of that neighbouring country.

As soon as these measures were known in America, the general indignation, irritated yet further by the reinforcement of the royal troops in Boston, and by various unpleasant circumstances and oppressions, inseparable from this event, was raised to the highest and most dangerous pitch. Instantaneously, through all the colonies but one voice was heard; that the contest with England could be decided only by the sword. Preparations for the most resolute defence were every where the great occupation; exercises of arms became the sole employment of the citizens. A congress of fifty-one deputies from all the provinces assembled on the 4th of September, 1774, at Philadelphia, to consult upon the common grievances, and upon the means of averting the common danger. The first measures of this assembly consisted in a solemn declaration, that the unjust and oppressive proceeding of parliament against the town of Boston, and the province of Massachusetts-Bay, was to be considered as the cause of all the colonies; and in a recommendation to the inhabitants of North-America to suspend all commercial intercourse with Great-Britain, until the just grievances of the colonies should be redressed. Hereupon, the congress resolved upon an address to the British nation, and another to the king of England, in which the distressed situation of North America was delineated with boldness and energy, but at the same time with evident moderation, and in a language, which still deprecated a separation from the mother country, as a very great evil.

It could no longer be concealed to the dullest eye, that the contest with the colonies had assumed a new and formidable character, and had spread to such an extent, as threatened the whole British empire. Yet, nothing is more certain, than that at this decisive moment, it still depended upon the parliament to finish it happily. No resolution, less than that of a total repeal of all the laws, promulgated since 1766, was commensurate with the greatness of the danger; but the thought that the immediate loss of America was at stake, should have reconciled every mind to this only remaining mean of salvation. Unfortunately, the deep exasperation, the inflexible pride, the false ambition, all the angry passions, which this cruel system had introduced and nourished, maintained now likewise their predominance; and a fatal error, the opinion that the victory over the colonies would be infallible and easy, entered into an unholy league with all those passions. The parliament, at the beginning of the year 1775, in a remarkable address to the king, declared, that both houses, convinced that a formal rebellion had broken out in the province of Massachusetts-Bay, would faithfully support him in every measure against rebellious subjects. Immediately afterwards, several laws of unmerciful severity, by which the colonies were deprived of all foreign commerce, and, what was yet harder, even of that fishery upon the coasts of Newfoundland so highly essential to their subsistence, passed by great majorities. Some of the wisest and most venerable statesmen, lord Chatham,* lord Camden,

* This great man, who, faithful to the principles of antient policy, and animated with the most unbounded zeal for the glory and welfare of his country, which under his administration had reached the zenith of her greatness, considered the separation of the colonies from England, as the greatest of all evils, said among other things, in a most impressive speech, with which on the 20th of January, 1775, he introduced the motion for withdrawing the troops from Boston. "I announce it to you now, my lords, we shall one day be *compelled* to repeal these oppressive regulations, they *must* be repealed; you

lord Shelburne, in the upper house, Edmund Burke,[18] colonel Barré, and others in the house of commons, exerted in vain against these desperate resolutions, all the powers of an astonishing eloquence; such as perhaps had never been surpassed. The several plans of conciliation, which they proposed, were rejected,

---

yourselves will retract them. I pledge myself for it; I stake my reputation upon it; I am content to pass for a blockhead, if they are not retracted."

It is furthermore very remarkable, that the disapprobation of the measures against America, was not confined to the then *opposition parties,* but was equally shown by several of the principal ministers. The duke of Grafton, who from 1766, to 1770, was first lord of the treasury, and afterwards, from 1771, to 1775, keeper of the seals, had at all times declared himself against the prevailing system; the same sentiments were ascribed to the earl of Dartmouth, secretary of state for America; lord North himself, who from 1770, was considered as first minister, is said to have manifested often in the deliberations of the cabinet, different principles from those he afterwards supported in parliament. But nothing can be more surprising, than that in one of the most violent debates, which took place in the house of lords, in February 1775, even lord Mansfield, a man in high consideration, and of great talents, but whom the whig party considered as an exaggerated partizan of the crown's rights, and as one of the most decided enemies of the Americans, carried away by the heat of the contest, formally declared, that the introduction of imposts, in the year 1767, was the most *absurd* and most *pernicious* measure that could have been devised, and had been the real cause of all the subsequent misfortunes.

always with displeasure, sometimes with contempt; the only step towards peace that ever was attempted, rested upon a project of lord North, evidently incompetent to the end; which would scarcely have satisfied the colonies at the outset of the dispute, and certainly could not content them in the year 1775.

The congress assembled, for the second time, in May, 1775, and declared, "that by the violation of the charter of Massachusetts-Bay, the connection between that colony and the crown was dissolved." The conciliatory bills of lord North were rejected; a *continental army* and a *paper currency* were created; colonel Washington was appointed commander in chief of the American troops, &c. The war at this period had, in fact, broken out; it had been opened by the battle of Lexington,[19] on the 19th of April, and while the congress were adopting these resolutions, a second and much bloodier action took place at Bunker's hill, where the loss suffered by the English army gave a severe, though unfortunately, a fruitless lesson to those, who had treated with so much contempt the resistance, and the military talents of the Americans.

Although every hope of peace had now well nigh vanished, the Congress were not however so far discouraged, as to decline venturing, even at this period, a last attempt at conciliation. They resolved a second address to the king, in which the colonies under the most forcible assurances of their submission, and of their unabated wish to remain united with Great Britain, intreated in the most urgent manner, that his majesty would give his assent to any plan whatsoever, calculated to pacify this wretched contest. The address was presented on the 1st. of September 1775, by Mr. Penn, of Pennsylvania,[20] one of the most respectable citizens of North America, who was informed "that no answer would be given to it." Soon after the minister brought into parliament the law, which prohibited all intercourse with the colonies, and declared their ships to be lawful prize; a law, which was justly considered as a declaration of war against America, and by some as a formal abdication of the right of government over the colonies. At the same time, the king concluded alliances with several German princes, who engaged their troops for a great undertaking; and preparations of every kind announced that force alone was to decide the destiny of the British empire. At the close of the session of parliament in February 1776, the bitterness had attained its highest pitch. Even the evident danger, that foreign powers, and France in particular, might take a part in the disturbances in America, and take advantage of England's embarrassment, made no impression upon the ministers and the parliament. When some members of the opposition at the beginning of the year 1776, asserted that according to very authentic accounts, a negociation between the Congress at Philadelphia, and the French court, was already commenced, not only the truth, but even the possibility of this but too well grounded fact was denied. It was maintained "that, such an unexampled fascination," could not be supposed in any nation, "holding colonies itself, in any government wishing to retain the obedience of their own subjects." A reasoning, which in itself rested upon very just principles, but which lost all its conclusive *weight* in the mouth of those, who, by a fascination entirely similar, had come to the point of setting at stake, from mere stupid obstinacy, one of their most precious possessions, and half the existence of their empire.

Since the last months of the year 1775, the war was raging in the bowels of the colonies. The language and the resolves of Parliament in the winter of 1775–1776, taught the Americans that it would be a war for life and death—Every bond of union was broken. Against the return of the old happy days the iron hand of inexorable destiny had barred every gate. On the 4th of July 1776, the Congress declared the Independence of the Thirteen United States.

It belongs not to the purpose of the present essay to continue further this cursory historical recapitulation, since I am here speaking only of the *origin* of the American revolution. It is however sufficiently known, that the *progress* and the *issue* of the war, completely justified the anticipations of those, who would have avoided it *at any price.* It is equally well known, how much the *consequences* of this war, have put to shame the expectations of all parties. The supporters of the war, went upon the principle, that every thing must be hazarded to maintain the possession of the colonies, its opponents, upon the principle that every thing must be *sacrificed* not to lose them; both concurred therefore in the opinion that this loss would give a deep, and perhaps incurable wound to the British empire. Experience has decided. In a few years after the loss of the colonies, England has again become as powerful and flourishing, nay more powerful and flourishing than ever.[21] And whatever of a hurtful nature, that lay in the influence of this event upon the affairs of Europe, has fallen upon *France* alone; upon France, who, according to the general opinion, was to derive the greatest advantages from the American revolution.

If we duly meditate upon the series of facts, which have been here summarily exhibited, and upon some others equally certain and authentic, which will be touched upon in the sequel, the following points of comparison will arise, to show in its clearest light the *essential* difference between the American and French revolutions.

1. The American revolution was grounded partly upon principles, of which the right *was evident,* partly upon such, as it was at least very questionable, whether they were not right, and from beginning to end upon no one that was clearly and decidedly wrong; the French revolution was an uninterrupted series of steps, the wrong of which could not, upon rigorous principles, for a moment be doubted.

The question, concerning the *right* of a revolution, has, by the frivolous way of thinking, by the shallow

sophistry, and even by the immense devastations, and
the stupid indifference arisen from them, of this revolutionary age, been in a manner discarded among the
idle amusements of scholastic pedants; many who hold
themselves for statesmen, think it no longer *worth while
so much as* to start the question; yet in the eyes of the
thinking, of the wise and the good, will it ever remain,
the first and the last.[22]

The relation between the inhabitants of a distant
colony, and the government of the mother country,
is never to be compared in all respects with the relation between the government and their immediate
subjects. In the former, there lies always something
strained, something equivocal, something unnatural; for it cannot be denied, the firmest foundation
of all sovereignty is in the wants of the governed, and
those wants are weaker, are more questionable, with-
draw themselves, to express myself so, from the eyes
and the feeling, when the government is a thousand
leagues distant from the country, which must obey
their laws. Besides, all the European states, which
founded, or encouraged the foundation of colonies
in the other quarters of the globe, considered these
colonies, more or less, as mere instruments to *en-
rich* and strengthen the seat of their own power, and
treated the people, who inhabited them, merely as
the means of an happier, or more agreeable existence
for their own. A maxim, which could not easily be
reconciled with the general purposes of society, for

which the colonies must have as keen a sense as the mother country, and with the consciousness of independent stability, to which they must sooner or later attain. Hence, the right of an European nation over their colonies must necessarily always be a wavering, insecure, undefined, and often undefinable right. If, however, the form of government in the mother country be simple, and the conditions, upon which the colony was founded, were in themselves clear and definite, then that unavoidable misrelation will be less perceptible. The difficulties on the other hand must be much greater, the collisions more frequent and momentous, when the mother country has a complicated constitution, and when the conditions under which the colonies are connected with her, the rights, which they enjoy by virtue of her particular constitution, the place which they are to hold in that constitution, are not in the precisest manner defined at their very origin.

This was in both points the case with the English colonies, in North America. How far the rights and liberties of a new state, founded by Britons, under the British constitution, should extend, and in what particular relation the inhabitants of such a state should stand, with the several component parts of that mixed constitution? this was a question, which at their origin should have been considered with the utmost attention. This question was never once thought of. The colonies originated at a time, when the British constitution itself had not yet attained its last perfection and consistence.* Their charters all proceeded from the *crown*. The parliament had never taken any part in their settlement.[23]

The internal forms of government of these colonies were as various, as the circumstances, under which they had been founded, or formed. Some of the most important had been granted as hereditary property to private persons, so that these, and their heirs, might govern them entirely as they pleased, and were scarcely more than under a nominal dependence upon the crown. In this manner had Maryland been granted to lord Baltimore; North and South-Carolina to lord Clarendon; in this manner Pennsylvania and Delaware belonged to the family of the celebrated Penn. Others, as New-Hampshire, New-York, New-Jersey, and Virginia, were called royal provinces, and in these the king was considered as the immediate sovereign. Lastly, there was a third class of colonies, which were called privileged, and in which the power of the monarch was limited

---

* Most of the colonies were founded before the middle of the seventeenth century; all before the revolution of 1688. The province of Georgia, the most southern of the colonies, and which was originally part of South Carolina, was the only one, which received her *separate* constitution since the beginning of this century (in 1732); and was likewise the only one for the settlement and cultivation of which the British government had been at any cost.

by the original charters. Such was the constitution of Massachusetts, of Rhode Island, and of Connecticut.

The relations between the royal governors, and the provincial assemblies, were in every colony differently defined and modified; but the provincial assemblies were accustomed every where, whether the province was originally privileged, royal, or hereditary, more or less, to exercise the right of enacting laws for the internal police of the province, of levying taxes for meeting the public exigences of the state, and of taking an essential part in every thing belonging to the administration of the country. In no single colony, however its constitution, in respect to its dependance upon the crown, was organized, was there a trace of a constitutional and legal authority, vested in the British parliament. The charters contained none; no definite law, not so much as a partial statute, enacted in Great-Britain, had ever proclaimed, or even made mention of such an authority.

In the beginning, the parliament considered this their absolute exclusion from the sovereignty over the colonies with great indifference; in the preceding century, the bounds of their power in general were so little defined, that not the smallest doubt has been started against the authority of the king, at his pleasure to give, to grant, to constitute, to privilege, to govern, by himself, or allow to be governed by others, an immense continent in America; this distant and uncultivated land, was besides far too much despised for them to concern themselves about its constitution. But when, on the one side, after the revolution of 1688,[24] the influence of parliament upon all the affairs of government had become greater, firmer, and more general; and when, on the other side, the extraordinary importance of the colonies, in their rapidly growing population, in their constantly improving culture, in their unexpected and splendid flourishing state, was daily more evident, the idea by degrees crept into every mind, that so great and essential a part of the British empire could not possibly be altogether withdrawn from the superintendency of parliament, even though nothing should have been said of it hitherto in the public transactions.

In one single, though truly important point, the parliament had always exercised the legislative power over the colonies, in every thing which concerned trade, whether of export, or of import. Although this was precisely the seat of that mighty monopoly, which seemed to give the colonies their whole value, and which, on the other side, could never be so favourable to their progress as liberty would have been, yet they willingly submitted to the regulations and restraints of all kinds, with which the parliament in ample measure provided them. It appeared natural and equitable to themselves, that the supreme legislative power in the empire, should regulate and direct a concern, which interested not exclusively America, but England too, in a much higher degree. The right of the parliament, therefore, to prescribe laws to the colonies relating to commerce, and to every thing connected with it, was never called in question.

But, as soon as the parliament determined to overstep this right, and to levy taxes in America, without the consent of the local representatives, the most ve- hement resistance could not fail to break out, and this resistance could as little fail to increase, when, in the progress of the contest, the pretention to bind Amer- ica by act of parliament, in all cases whatsoever, was advanced, and formally derived from what was called the legal supremacy of parliament. The *omnipotence* of parliament, so often, and so loudly, then resounded by the antagonists of the colonies, was a very just prin- ciple for England, but a very invalid one for America. With the parliament, bating the trade laws, to which the colonists submitted from reason and necessity, America had not the least to do. America sent no rep- resentatives to parliament, nor did it ever occur to par- liament to offer her that power, which would indeed not have been without great difficulties carried into effect. The colonies, nevertheless, possessed all the benefits of the British constitution, and even the great- est part of their forms. Almost in every one of them, there was a *representative assembly,* which supplied the place of a lower house, and a senate, which answered to the house of peers. These assemblies transacted, un- der the sanction of the monarch, all the affairs, which in England and Ireland were done by the parliaments. They enacted laws, levied taxes, deliberated upon the exigencies, and upon the administration of their prov- inces. They formed, in concurrence with the king and his governors, a complete government, organized al- together in the spirit of the English constitution, and needed no co-operation of the British parliament. The constitutions of the several provinces, knew only the king, and the provincial representative bodies, and had no more reference to the parliament of Great-Britain, than to the parliaments of France. They had existed more than a century, without knowing any thing of the English parliament, otherwise than by its commercial regulations, which had not always been to them the most agreeable. The pretended right of parliament to prescribe laws and taxes for them, was an arbitrary assumption, against which the colonies, according to all legal principles, might proceed exactly as Great-Britain would have done, had any of the provincial assemblies undertaken, with the concurrence of the king, to levy taxes in England or Scotland, or to overthrow the municipal constitution of London or Westminster, as the parliament had overthrown the charter of Massachusetts-Bay.

The resistance of the colonies, and the unavoidable insurrection, which was finally produced by the continuance of the attack, were, therefore, inasmuch as they respected the parliament, perfectly *right*. The parliament was, in regard to the colonies, to be considered as a *foreign power*. So long as this power had remained within the bounds of its silently acknowledged sphere of operation, the colonies had submitted to it. To give laws beyond those bounds, it was as little authorised, as would have been the legislative power of any other nation. The Americans could resist it with the same right, as they might have resisted the States-General of

Holland, or the council of the Indies in Madrid, had these undertaken to impose upon them their manufacturing regulations, or stamp taxes.

The question seems to be more difficult, with what right the colonies could likewise resist the king, who, at any rate, was their legal and acknowledged sovereign? But, if in this respect the lawfulness of their conduct be doubtful, it would at least remain a great point, that its unlawfulness could not be clearly proved, and a closer examination will lead us to a result yet far more favourable to the justification of this conduct.

For there is a very evident distinction between an insurrection in a *simple,* and one in a *complicated,* or *mixed constitution.* In a simple government, every resistance against the supreme power, is absolutely illegal, and requires no further examination to be condemned. In a mixed government, cases may be imagined, in which the matter is very intricate, and therefore problematic and dubious.

In a mixed government, the supreme power, or the proper sovereign, consists always of several component parts connected together and regulated by the constitution. Each of these parts has its constitutional rights and prerogatives; and those of any one part, though in themselves more important, cannot be more sacred than those of any other. When either of them exceeds its legal bounds, and oppresses, or endeavours to destroy another, this latter, unless the constitution be an empty name, must have the right of resisting; and, unless the war, arising from this resistance, be not averted by some fortunate expedient; if the old balance cannot again be restored, the contest must necessarily, and *legally* end with the dissolution of the constitution. For between two independent component parts of the supreme power in a state, there can no more be a judge, than between two independent states. That this is a most unfortunate situation for the whole nation, interested in it, is self evident. The most dreadful circumstance it brings with it, is unquestionably this, that the people in such a controversy never know whom to obey, and whom to resist; for whom to declare, and against whom to act; that all rights and duties are thrown into confusion, and involved in obscurity, and that it becomes a problem, who is within, and who is without the line of insurrection. This evil is inseparable from mixed forms of government;* and however great it may be, its possibil-

* This is undoubtedly the greatest failing that can be objected against mixed governments. Fortunately, however, it must be acknowledged, that the probability of such a dissolution is more remote in proportion as the constitution approaches nearer to perfection. For the more easily one of the constituted authorities can resist the other, by its appropriate weight, the less will be the necessity of appealing to arms. On the other hand, the more imperfect the balance is, the greater will be the danger of a civil war. In this lies properly the decided superiority of the British constitution, above all other complicated forms of government, that ever were, or probably ever will be devised.

ity can never be excluded from such constitutions. If, for example, the two houses of the British parliament should make the attempt to enact laws, without the sanction of the king, or the king, without the concurrence of parliament, the injured party would beyond all doubt resist, and resist with energy; nor could any one deny that this resistance, even though it should end in civil war and the ruin of the constitution, was perfectly lawful.

The American colonies were precisely in this, or at least in an extremely similar situation. Their constitution before the revolution was evidently a monarchy, more or less limited by the influence of their provincial assemblies. The legislative and executive powers were divided between the king and the provincial assemblies, as in England, between the king and the two houses of parliament. The king and his governor had only a negative upon acts of legislation, and the provincial assemblies in most of the colonies had a considerable share in the government. In all the provinces (Pennsylvania since 1700 excepted) these assemblies were divided into two houses, closely corresponding in their functions, with the two branches of the British parliament. The lower house, or the representative assembly possessed every where the exclusive right of prescribing taxes. In some colonies, for instance, in Maryland, the king, by the charter, *had expressly* renounced all right of taxation. In several others he had, in the literal sense of the word, only reserved the empty title of sovereignty. Connecticut and Rhode-

Island were perfect democracies. The colonial assemblies of these provinces chose their governors without the confirmation of the king, and dismissed them at pleasure; they allowed no appeals from their courts of justice; their laws required no royal assent; nay, what is more remarkable, and a proof of their absolute independence, their charters granted them even the right of peace and war.[25]

The king's power was, therefore, in all the colonies, more or less limited; in some, to such a degree that it could not be compared with his legitimate power in Great-Britain; and the colonial assemblies had a constitutional right to resist him, when he violated their constitutional powers. Now, the measures of the ministry, from 1764, were evident attacks, upon those powers. Whether the parliament had advised, or confirmed those attacks, was, as we have before shewn, nothing to the colonies; they had to do only with the king, and the king, according to their constitutions, could levy no taxes, but such as the provincial assemblies proposed. The stamp-act of 1764, was, therefore, a violation of their rights; the impost act of 1767, was a violation of their rights; the act of 1770, which maintained the tea-tax to support the supremacy of parliament, was a gross, and what was worst of all, an insulting violation of their rights. To punish them for their constitutional resistance against these unconstitutional resolves, was a revolting injustice; the mode of punishment (the Boston port-bill, the bill to abolish the Massachusetts charter, &c.) was not merely a violation, it was an entire dissolution of their rights. It was nothing more, than the proclamation of a *fact,* when the congress, in 1775, declared, "that by the abolition of the Massachusetts charter, *the connection between that province and the crown was dissolved.*" No resource was left but that of repelling force by force. The convocation of their first congress, was in itself not an illegal measure. This congress exercised originally only the same rights, which were unquestionably within the powers of every provincial assembly. It represented a legal resistance, and sought the means of preserving to America the constitution she had hitherto possessed. It was not until after the ministry had spurned at peace, rejected every proposal of conciliation, and finally required unconditional submission, that is, had *dissolved the constitution,* that the congress proceeded to the declaration, which substituted a new government, in the stead of that which was destroyed.

Had the colonies had the design (and it cannot be denied that they manifested it clearly enough) in this whole contest to separate the king completely from the parliament, all the means were taken away from them of regulating their conduct, according to a system founded upon such a separation. The most intimate union subsisted between the ministry and the parliament; nor was it possible to resist the one, without quarrelling with the other. The king confirmed the hostile acts of parliament; he ceased to be the constitutional monarch of the colonies, and entered into an alliance with those, whom they considered as usurpers in a legal point of view.[26] Had the king of England allied himself with a foreign power (and in a constitutional sense the parliament was no other to the colonies) against the parliament of Great-Britain, how would it be possible for the parliament to arm against this foreign power, and yet spare the king of England? Or rather, would not the mere undertaking of such an alliance include within itself an immediate justification of every defensive measure taken by the injured party, and an absolute renunciation of the constitution.

I think I have here sufficiently developed the first point in the comparison I proposed, that which relates to the conduct of North-America; there now remains only the easy task of exhibiting the second, which relates to the conduct of France.

The single period of the disturbances in France, when mention was made of militating *rights,* was that in which the parliaments took part, in 1787 and 1788. If the prerogatives of these parliaments were not so great and so unquestionable, as they would have represented them, yet their appeal to them gave at least a colour of lawfulness to their undertakings. That period, however, is to be considered only as preparatory to the real revolution.[27]

From the breaking out of this revolution, the question as to the *lawfulness* of what the popular leaders did, was never (an extraordinary, yet an indubitable fact!) started. The word *right* would have vanished from the French language, had not an imaginary right of the *nation,* to do whatever they, or their representatives should please, appeared as a sort of substitute for all other rights.

This is not the place to analyse this *right of the nation,* sometimes likewise called *right of man,* a sort of magic spell, with which all the ties of nations and of humanity were insensibly dissolved. Those, who were serious in advancing, grounded it upon the chimerical principle of the sovereignty of the people, which I have endeavoured upon another occasion to elucidate. Thus much is certain, that the leaders of the revolution, under the shelter of this talisman, spared themselves and others the trouble of enquiring into the lawfulness of their proceedings; for in their system, all was right, which they resolved upon in the name of the *people,* or in the name of mankind.

In order to judge of their actions, according to their deserts, they must be snatched away from the tribunal they have erected for themselves, and placed at another bar, whose laws accord better with the dictates of uncorrupted reason, and the eternal prescriptions of *real right.*

When the deputies of the states, assembled together in the year 1789, they had beyond all doubt the *right,* to undertake great reforms in the government, and even in the constitution of the French monarchy. This right, however, they could exercise only under the three following conditions. First, that they should observe the general forms of an assembly of the states in France, until these forms should in a *lawful* manner be abolished, or changed. Secondly, that their laws should not have the force of laws, until assented to by the monarch. And, thirdly, that they should follow the instructions, given them by their constituents.

In less than six weeks, they had broken through these three fundamental conditions. The deputies of the third state, without the least authority, and with a shameful violation of the rights of the other states, declared that themselves alone constituted the national assembly.

When the king endeavoured to bring them back from this monstrous usurpation to their proper limits, they declared to him that they persisted in it, formally renounced obedience to him, and reduced him finally to the necessity of commanding the two other estates to acknowledge the usurpation.

That in the immeasurable career, which these two first successful acts of violence, had opened, they might no longer meet resistance from any quarter, they declared that the instructions of their constituents were not binding upon them.

They had proceeded thus far, when, partly by their influence and example, partly by faults of the court, which need not be considered here, where the question only relates to *right,* the general rebellion broke out in Paris, and in all the provinces. Far from *disapproving* this rebellion, which, in perfect contrast with the rising of the people in America, had not the most distant connection with the lawful objects of the national assembly, they cherished and fostered it, gave it legislative force and consistence, conferred civic crowns upon its authors, called it an holy and virtuous insurrection, and took care to have it maintained in a continual flame, during the whole period of their government.

Under the shadow of this insurrection, they, who had placed themselves at its head, and taken upon themselves all responsibility, in a period of two years ran through the most remarkable circle of violation of all rights, public and private, that the world ever beheld. They drew up, without ever so much as *asking the free assent of the king,* a constitution so called, the incompetency, the impracticability, the ridiculous absurdity of which was so great, that, even among its authors—(another unexampled yet indubitable fact) not a single man would ever have seriously defended it. This constitution they compelled the king, upon pain of being immediately dethroned, to subscribe and swear to.

Scarcely had this happened, when their successors, who by virtue of this constitution alone, had a sort of legal existence, and held something resembling an authority to shew, instead of governing and quieting the state according to this constitution, directed all their secret, and what was still more revolting, all their public measures to its destruction. In less than a year they succeeded in effecting this new usurpation. Without so much as having a *legal pretext,* they suspended the constitution, dethroned the king, assumed to themselves, still forsooth *in the name of the people,* the power of calling a *national convention,* and proclaimed the republic, with fewer formalities, than a man would use to change his dress. By long habit dead to every sentiment of *right,* tormented by all the furies, plunged by their frantic measures, by crimes, and calamities of every kind into the lowest depth of criminal fool-hardiness, they now proclaimed against humanity and all its rights, a formal, irreconcileable war; and to shut behind them every door for return, and to snap the last thread by which they still held together with a lawful existence, they finally murdered justice herself, in the person of the most conscientious and upright monarch, who had ever adorned a throne.[28]

The French revolution, therefore, began by a violation of rights, every step of its progress was a violation of rights, and it was never easy, until it had succeeded to establish absolute wrong, as the supreme and acknowledged maxim of a state completely dissolved, and yet existing only in bloody ruins.

2. The American revolution was from beginning to end, on the part of the Americans, merely a *defensive revolution;* the French was from beginning to end, in the highest sense of the word, *an offensive revolution.*

This difference of itself is essential and decisive; upon it rests, perhaps more than upon any other, the peculiar character, which has distinguished these two revolutions.

The British government began the revolution in America by resolves, for which they could shew no right; the colonies endeavoured by all means in their power to repel them. The colonies wished to maintain their old constitution; the government destroyed it. The resistance, which the colonies opposed against the mother country, was, in every period of this unhappy contest, exactly commensurate with the attack; the total separation was not resolved, until the utter impossibility of preserving the ancient condition was proved.

The stamp-act threw America into the most violent commotion; tumultuous scenes, though attended with no acts of bloody violence, broke out in all the provinces.* But they were no where formally sanctioned by the approbation of the legislative authorities. The little congress of 28 deputies of several colonies, who in the year 1765 assembled at New-York, and served as the model for the subsequent larger assembly, passed no other resolution than that "the colonies could only be taxed by their representatives," and expressed this perfectly lawful resolve, in *petitions* to the king. The single general measure, which was then offered, the non-importation agreement, was a voluntary engagement, sanctioned by no public authority.

The *declaratory act,* which appeared in the year 1766, together with the repeal of the stamp-tax, could not possibly be agreeable to the colonies since it expressly and solemnly maintained the right of the British parliament to bind them by law in all cases whatsoever. Yet was this act received with great and remarkable tranquillity; and had the British government, from

* In many places the public officers appointed to collect the stamp-tax, were hanged up, or beheaded; but all, only in *effigy.*

that time forward, given up forever their unhappy innovations; had they continued to govern the colonies,
according to the old constitutional principles, there
never would have been uttered a complaint against
the declaratory act. It was long afterwards, and when
the colonies had been provoked by repeated attacks of
every kind, to the utmost extremity, that the provincial
assembly of Massachusetts-Bay, declared that statute,
an oppression.

The resistance against the impost taxes of 1767, was
of the same nature, as that which the stamp-tax had
experienced. This new grievance of the colonies, was
accompanied with circumstances of the most odious
kind: the augmentation of the troops, the conduct
of a part of them, the harshness of some governors,
the frequent adjournments and violent dissolution of
the provincial assemblies, all was calculated to put the
patience of the Americans to dangerous proof. And
yet they never overstepped the boundaries, which the
constitution and the laws prescribed to them; and in
their numerous addresses and protestations, adhered
rigorously to what was allowed by law. When in the
year 1770, a violent quarrel arose between some of the
royal soldiers, and certain citizens of Boston, which
ended in the first bloody scene the colonies had in
their contest with England yet witnessed, the courts of
law, with a glorious impartiality, acquitted the greatest
part of the accused and indicted soldiers.

The continuation of the tax upon tea in the year
1770, had no other consequence than to strengthen

the voluntary agreement against the importation of English tea; the resolve in the year 1773, which authorised the East-India company to the exportation of their stores of tea, free from duty, and the actual execution of this resolve, could not, indeed but produce a still more unfavourable operation. This measure was altogether calculated to provoke the colonies to a general insurrection. Yet did they keep themselves rigorously within the limits of a necessary defence. The destruction of the tea at Boston was, in fact, no other than a defensive operation. The sale of this tea, or only a part of it, would have involved the compulsive levy of a tax, by the payment of which the constitution of the colonies and all their rights would have been lost. Yet, even then, they proceeded not beyond what was unavoidable, and measured the resistance as exactly as possible by the attack. The tea was thrown into the sea, and not a single hostile step followed upon this undertaking. Nay, although the public authorities of Boston, and of the whole province, held it for necessary, as much as every single citizen, yet they always undeniably discovered themselves ready to grant the fullest indemnity to the East-India company.

Had the ministry, at this period, been contented with an equitable satisfaction; had they, if they must punish, been content to inflict tolerable and proportionable punishments, there is no doubt but America would have remained with her old constitution. Although a great part of the inhabitants of the colonies, in expectation of a distressing and stormy futurity, urged for energy and for arming, yet was this temper still far from being common. It is, for example, a certain fact, that in the important province of Pennsylvania, the majority of the citizens would have voted against taking a part in the measures at Boston, had not the excessive and unwise harshness of the parliament, in a short time, inflamed and united all minds.

The appearance of the act, which closed the port of Boston, of that which, immediately after, took away the Massachusetts charter, the account of all what had passed in parliament upon that occasion, the visible impossibility of eradicating peaceably such deep rooted bitterness—all these circumstances concurred to render a sudden explosion probable; many of the resolves of parliament were indisputably of a nature to furnish sufficient motive for such an explosion. But the provincial assemblies contented themselves with sending deputies to a general congress. Not one over hasty step disturbed the pacific and lawful character of their conduct in this hard and trying period.

The congress, which assembled at Philadelphia,[29] spoke with energetic freedom of the constitutional rights of the colonies, and of the oppressive measures of parliament; but their first resolves were more moderate, than perhaps England herself had expected. An invitation to a general agreement against all trade with Great-Britain was the only active step they allowed themselves; and after all what the parliament had done, this step was of little importance. How far they were remote, even then, from a total separation, and how much the conduct of the colonies deserved the name of a lawful defence, may be learned from the following conclusion of the remarkable address, which this congress immediately before separating, sent to the king.

> We ask only for peace, liberty and security. We wish no dimi-nution of royal prerogatives, we demand *no new rights*. From the magnanimity and justice of your majesty, and the parlia-ment, we promise ourselves the redress of our grievances; firmly convinced, that when once the causes of our pres-ent complaints are removed, our future conduct will not be undeserving of the milder treatment, to which we were in better days accustomed. We call that Being, who tries the in-most heart, to witness, that no other motive, than the fear of the destruction, which threatens us, has had any influence upon our resolutions. We therefore intreat your majesty as the loving father of all your people, bound to you by the ties of blood, by laws, affection, and fidelity, not to permit, in the uncertain expectation of a result, which never can compen-sate for the wretchedness by which it must be attained, any further violation of those sacred ties. So may your majesty in a long and glorious reign, enjoy every earthly bliss, and this bliss, and your undiminished authority descend upon your heirs and their heirs, till time shall be no more.

The American agents in London, Bollan, Franklin and Lee, petitioned to be heard in support of this ad-dress, at the bar of the parliament. Their request was rejected.

Soon after, this cruel act, which deprived the colo-nies of all navigation, and even of the fishery, obtained the force of law; and the very moment, when this harsh law was past, was chosen to make the only proposal of conciliation, which the parliament had ever offered. According to this proposal, which is known by the name of lord North's Conciliatory Plan,[30] every colony, whose representatives would engage to deliver their proportional contribution to the exigencies of the empire, and raise besides the costs of their internal administration, *provided* their offers should be approved by the king and parliament, was to be secured in the exemption from all further taxation. Not to mention that the only object of this plan notoriously was to divide the colonies, that it was offered them by an armed hand, that the *suspicious proviso* made the favourable consequences of its acceptance extremely doubtful, it properly decided the true point of contest, in a manner wholly contradictory to the principles of the Americans. The parliament renounced a right which notoriously did not belong to them. But they renounced it, only to exercise, once for all, what they had wished to exercise by piece-meal. The injustice and inconsistency of this proposal could not for a moment escape the notice of the colonies. The second general congress, which assembled on the 10th of May, 1775,[31] rejected it upon grounds, the force of which must be felt by every impartial mind. "Should we accede," say they, in their answer to this proposal,

we should expressly declare a wish to purchase the favour of parliament, without knowing at what price it would be set. We hold it superfluous to extort from us, by violence or threats a proportional contribution, to meet the general exigencies of the state, since all the world knows, and the parliament must themselves acknowledge, that whenever thereto required, in a constitutional manner, we have always richly contributed. It is unjust to require permanent contributions of the colonies, so long as Great-Britain possesses the monopoly of their trade; this monopoly is, in itself, the heaviest of all contributions. It is unjust to wish to tax us doubly. If we must contribute in like proportion with the other parts of the empire, allow us, like them too, a free trade with all the world.

These unanswerable arguments were at an immeasurable distance from the language of insolent rebellion.

When, finally, the congress resolved upon the general arming of the country, *defence* was still their single, and exclusive object. The constitution had been long since, without their fault, torn to pieces; they might have proclaimed immediately a new one upon its ruins; but they appealed to arms, to maintain the same constitution, of which the colonies had been, with so much violence, deprived.

The surest proof of this glorious moderation was, that they themselves, after the actual breaking out of hostilities, and when a great part of the inhabitants of America, urged for more energetic measures, did not omit another attempt by petitions and remonstrances, to attain the end of their wishes. In the midst of the most vigorous preparations for a desperate defence, they resolved, in the month of July, 1775,* another address to the king, to which was given the inviting and significant name of the *olive branch*. Even in this last address, we read with astonishment, among other things, as follows:

> Devoted to the person, the family, and the government of your majesty, with all the attachment, which only principle and feeling can inspire, connected with Great-Britain, by the strongest ties that can unite human societies together, deeply afflicted at every event that may weaken this connection, we most solemnly assure your majesty, *that we wish nothing more ardently than the restoration of the former harmony* between England and the colonies, and a new union, founded upon a lasting basis, capable of propagating that blessed harmony to the latest generations, and transmit to a grateful posterity your majesty's name, surrounded with that immortal glory which was in every age bestowed upon the saviours of the people. We protest to your majesty, that

* Shortly before, the congress are said to have resolved upon a declaration, by virtue of which, the colonies offered, "not only for the future, in time of war, to pay extraordinary contributions, but likewise, provided they were allowed a free trade, for an hundred years, to pay an annual sum, sufficient in that period to extinguish the whole British national debt," and to have been deterred from giving their last sanction to this declaration, only by the account of new hostile measures of the parliament. This highly remarkable fact I mention however only upon the authority of a single writer, a very severe antagonist of the ministry, though otherwise very well informed. Belsham's Memoirs of George III. Vol. 2. p. 166.[32]

notwithstanding all our sufferings in this unhappy contest, the hearts of your faithful colonists are far from wishing a reconciliation upon conditions, which could be inconsistent with the dignity, or the welfare of the state from which they sprung, and which they love with filial tenderness. If the grievances, which now bow us down with inexpressible pain to the ground, could in any manner be removed, your majesty will at all times find your faithful subjects in America, willing and ready, with their lives and fortunes, to maintain, preserve, and defend the rights and interests of their sovereign, and of their mother country.

This was the address, which Mr. Penn, on the 1st of September, 1775, delivered to the earl of Dartmouth, upon which, some days after, he was informed, *that no answer could be given.* It was not until after this last attempt had proved fruitless, after an unmerciful statute had outlawed American ships, and the levying of foreign troops left them only the choice between the dissolution of their constitution, with unconditional submission, and the same dissolution with the free choice of a new one, that the congress passed the resolve, which reason and necessity prescribed, and declared the colonies independent, because independence was a smaller evil than dependence upon arbitrary will; and their painfully maintained, and painfully defended dependence upon the old laws, was lost forever.

The revolution of America was, therefore, in every sense of the word, a revolution of necessity: England, alone, had by violence effected it: America had contended ten years long, not against England, but against the revolution: America sought not a revolution; she yielded to it, compelled by necessity, not because she wished to extort a better condition than she had before enjoyed, but because she wished to avert a worse one, prepared for her.

Exactly the contrary of all this, was the case in France. The French revolution was *offensive* in its origin, offensive in its progress, offensive in its whole compass, and in every single characteristic moment of its existence. As the American revolution had exhibited a model of moderation in defence, so the French one displayed an unparalleled example of violence and inexorable fury in attack. As the former had always kept the vigour of its defensive measures in rigorous proportion to the exigency, so the latter, from the weakness of the resistance made against it, became more and more violent and terrible, the more cause it had to grow milder.

Could the destroyers of a throne, could the teachers and heroes of a revolutionary age, themselves have formed the character of a prince, under whom they would begin their dreadful experiment, they never could have succeeded better, than in that, which a cruel destiny delivered into their hands. Lewis the 16th promoted the revolution by all the good, and by all the weak sides of his character.[33] He was certainly not equal to the circumstances, under which he had to act, and to the dangers, which he was to overcome; but what rendered his want of energy truly fatal, were his virtues. Had he been less honourable, less benevolent, less humane, less conscientious, perhaps he might yet have saved the monarchy. The unhappy certainty that it was impossible for him, so much as for a moment, to be a tyrant, made him and the state the victims of the most shameful and most revolting tyranny that the world had ever seen. His noble readiness to encourage every thing, which assumed the name of reform, drew him into the first false steps, which shook his throne. His horror of violence tore the sceptre from his benevolent hands. His integrity was the best ally of those, who plunged France and him into the precipice.

He looked with satisfaction towards that assembly of the states, whose effects had in the council of the wicked been long prepared. They rewarded him by the decrees, which excluded him from the government of the kingdom. He would not suffer his troops to use force against the first insurgents. They rewarded him by the general insurrection of the capital and of all the provinces. He endeavoured, even after having lost all his power, and tasted the bitterest afflictions, such as a dethroned monarch only can know, still to turn the evil to good. They improved this insurmountable royal temper, this pure and real civism,[34] to be guilty with less interruption, while he continued to hope; and to crush him with the load of their present crimes, while he looked forward to a better futurity.

It may boldly be maintained almost every thing that has been said of the resistance of the court and of the great, of their conspiracies, of their cabals against the revolution, was merely a wretched fable.

That the injured, the oppressed, the plundered could be no friends to their oppressors and plunderers is self-evident; as far as mere hatred is resistance, there was an enormous mass of resistance against the revolution; the leaders had themselves created these internal, these secret hostilities, of which they so often complained. They must have extirpated human nature herself to secure to themselves forgiveness, or a disposition to favour their cruel operations. But, throughout their whole career, they met with no active resistance, and the only circumstance, which could spread a varnish of credibility over their incessant fictions of plots, counter-revolutions, &c. was, that they *deserved* all, that they pretended to suffer.

If we follow this revolution through all its periods, we shall find that the strongest motive for effecting any greater usurpation, for maintaining any greater injustice, for committing any greater crime, constantly was, that a smaller one had immediately before succeeded. The single motive for using persecutions, was, that the victims had already suffered others. This was the character of the French revolution, in wholesale and in retail. The sufferers were punishable, merely because they had suffered; in this bitterest of all offensive wars, they seemed so cautiously to shun every thing that made a shew of resistance, that they sooner forgave a struggling, than a defenceless, enemy.

The relics of the old constitution were not so much boundaries to the omnipotent desolating power of the revolution, as land-marks, designating its victorious progress. The constitution, of 1791, was only a short and voluntary pause; a sort of resting point, at which nobody meant long to wait. The second national assembly did not make a pass, no, not one, which was not an attack upon some ruin or other of the monarchy. The establishment of the republic did not satisfy its authors. The execution of the king scarcely appeased the ravenousness of his butchers, for a single instant. In the year 1793 the thirst for destruction had gone so far, that it was at a loss for an object. The well known saying, that Robespierre meant to reduce the population of France by one half, had its foundation in the lively sense of the impossibility of satisfying the hitherto insatiate revolution, with any thing less, than such a hecatomb.[35]

When there was nothing more left in the country to attack, the offensive frenzy turned itself against the neighbouring states, and finally declared war in solemn decrees against all civil society. It was certainly not the want of will in those, who then conducted this war, if Europe preserved any thing, besides "bread and iron." Fortunately, no strength was great enough long to support such a will. The unavoidable exhaustion of the assailants, and not the power or the merit of the resistance made, saved society; and, finally, brought the work shops themselves, where the weapons for its destruction were forged, within its beneficent bonds again.

As the American revolution was a defensive revolution, it was of course finished, at the moment, when it had overcome the attack, by which it had been occasioned. The French revolution, true to the character of a most violent offensive revolution, could not but proceed so long as there remained objects for it to attack, and it retained strength for the assault.

3. The American revolution, at every stage of its duration, had a fixed and definite object, and moved within definite limits, and by a definite direction towards this object. The French revolution never had a definite object; and, in a thousand various directions, continually crossing each other, ran through the unbounded space of a fantastic arbitrary will, and of a bottomless anarchy.

It lay in the very nature of a defensive revolution, like that of America, to proceed from definite objects, and to pursue definite ends. The peculiar situation, and the peculiar character of the North-Americans confirmed and secured this moderate and beneficent quality to the progress of their revolution.

In the course of it, two principal periods may be observed; *that,* from the first breaking out of the contests in 1765, until the declaration of independence in 1776, and *that,* from this declaration, until the peace with England.

In the first period, the single towns and provinces, and afterwards the members of the general congress, had for their declared and sole object the salvation of their constitution, and of their rights and liberties, as they then stood, from the oppressive usurpations of the British parliament. And I think I have clearly shown, in the former sections of this essay, that every step they took, during that critical period was calculated for preservation, not for conquest, for resistance against innovations, not for ardour after them; for defence, not for attack.

In the second period, indeed, a new object came in the place of that, which they had until then pursued: the British parliament had compelled the congress to proclaim the independence of the colonies; but, even this decisive measure by no means threw America into the precipice of lawlessness, into the horrible gulph of an unmeasurable interregnum, or into the slippery career of wild and chimerical theories—The machine of government was, and remained, completely organized: the revolution had taken from the king his negative upon legislative acts, almost the only essential prerogative, which as sovereign of the colonies he immediately exercised: but every province took care that this important function should be performed by another authority, distinct from the legislature, and Georgia and Pennsylvania, were the only ones, which entrusted the legislative powers to an undivided senate. The royal governors, who till then had stood at the head of the executive power, were replaced by others, chosen by the provinces themselves; and as the former governors, owing to their great distance from the mother country, had always held powers in the highest degree discretionary and independent, this alteration could not be much felt—The great and immediate exigences of social life, the local administration, the police, and course of judicial proceeding were continued as before. Nothing but the loose tie, which had connected America with England, was broken; none of the internal relations were discomposed; all the laws remained in force; the condition of persons and of property suffered no other revolution, than that which was necessarily brought with it! "The people," says that very well informed American historian Dr. Ramsay,[36] "scarcely perceived that an alteration in their political constitution had taken place."

As the founders and conducters of the American revolution, from the beginning, knew exactly how far they were to go, and where they must stop; as the new existence of their country, the constitutions of the several provinces, and even the organization of the federal government, at least in its principles was definitely prescribed to them; as their purpose was in no sort to create, but only to preserve, not to erect a new building, but to free the old one from an external, burdensome, straitening scaffolding, and as it never occurred to them, in the rigorous sense of the word, to *reform*, even their own country, much less the whole world, they escaped the most dangerous of all the rocks, which in our times threaten the founders of any great revolution, the deadly passion for making political experiments with abstract theories, and untried systems. It is of the utmost importance, in judging the American revolution, never to lose sight of this point, and by so much the more important, as certain expressions in the early resolves of congress, the maxims of single writers, but especially the frequent appeals of the first leaders of the French revolution to the example of their predecessors in America, have encouraged, and spread abroad the opinion that these, in truth, opened the wide field of revolutionary speculations, and of systematic anarchy—True it is, that the declaration of independence published by the congress, in the name of the colonies, is proceeded by an introduction, in which the *natural* and *unalienable* rights of mankind are considered as the foundation of all government; that after this assertion, so indefinite, and so exposed to the greatest misconstructions, follow certain principles, no less indefinite, no less liable to be abused, from which an inference might be drawn of the unlimited right of the people to change their form of government, and what in the new revolutionary language, is called their *sovereignty.* It is likewise true, that most of the constitutions of the United States, are preceded by those idle *declaration of rights,* so dangerous in their application, from which so much misery has at a later period been derived upon France, and the whole civilized world.[37] Much, however, as it were to be wished, that the legislators of America had disdained this empty pomp of words, that they had exclusively confined themselves within the clear and lawful motives of their resistance; a resistance at first constitutional, and afterwards necessary, and within the limits of their uncontrovertible rights, yet it cannot escape the observation of those, who attentively study the history of their revolution, that they allowed to these speculative ideas, no visible influence upon their practical measures and resolves—They erroneously believed them necessary to justify their first steps;* but here the dominion of empty speculation, was forever abandoned—Never, in the whole course of the American revolution, were the *rights of man,* appealed to, for the destruction of the *rights of a citizen;* never was the sovereignty of the people used as a pretext to undermine the respect, due to the laws, or the foundations of social security; no example was ever seen of an individual, or a whole class of individuals, or even the representatives of this, or that single state, who recurred to the declaration of rights, to escape from positive obligation, or to renounce obedience to the common sovereign; finally, never did it enter the head of any legislator, or statesman in America, to combat the lawfulness of foreign constitutions, and to set up the American revolution, as a new epoch in the general relations of civil society.

What was here and there occasionally said by single writers, must carefully be distinguished from the principles and way of thinking of those Americans, who were acknowledged and revered as examples and authorities, but especially from those, who took an active part in the new government. There certainly was in America, a Thomas Paine;[38] and I will not deny but

---

* I believe that in the first section of this Essay, I have completely shown the lawfulness of the American revolution upon legal principles; and yet in that analysis, it will be found, that the sphere of unalienable rights of man, and the sovereignty of the people, and the like principles, are not once touched upon.

that his celebrated work had influence among certain classes of people, and so far contributed to promote the revolution.* But to judge of the spirit and principles of

* The general opinion, and the unanimous testimony of all the known writers upon American affairs, leave scarce room for a doubt of this fact, though for the honour of the Americans I would most willingly call it in question. His "*Common Sense,*" is a pamphlet just as contemptible, almost throughout just as remote from sound human sense, as all the others by which, in later times, he has made himself a name. To appreciate the character and tendency of this work, which, perhaps, has never been judged as it deserves, and to obtain a full conviction that it was solely calculated to make an impression upon the mass of the people, and especially upon certain religious sects very extensively spread in America, the reader has only to remark the spirit of the author's favourite arguments, which are all drawn from the *Old Testament,* and the absurd reasoning, with which he attacks, not the king of England, but monarchy in general, which he treats as an *ungodly* invention. If *such a work* could have produced the American revolution, it would have been best for reasonable men to concern themselves no longer with that event. But it was certainly at all times, by the wiser and better men, considered, endured, and perhaps encouraged, only as an instrument to gain over weaker minds to the common cause.

The difference between this writer and the great authorities of the American revolution, such as Dickenson, John Adams, Jay, Franklin,[39] &c. will be still more apparent, if we remark a similar difference between the two parties in England, which accidentally concurring in the same object, but differing infinitely from each other in the choice of means and arguments, declared themselves there in favour of that revolution. Whoever compares, for example, the writings of Dr. Price,[40] (who not-

the American revolution by this work, would be as unjust, as to confound the efficaciously active heads in the
English revolution, of 1688, with the authors of some
popular lampoon against the house of Stewart; or the
opposition of lord Chatham, with that of Mr. Wilkes.[42]

---

withstanding his numerous errors, deserves not, however, to be
put in the same class with Paine,) with the speeches and writings
of Burke during the American war, will sometimes be scarcely
able to convince himself, that both were contending for one
and the same thing. And, indeed, it was only nominally, and not
substantially, one and the same thing, for which they argued.

Another indirect, but not unimportant, proof of the accuracy and necessity of the distinction here pointed out, lies in
the unquestionable aversion of most of the great statesmen in
America to the French revolution, and to all what since 1789,
has been called revolutionary principles. A remarkable anec-
dote occurs, testified by a witness unobjectionable upon this
point, by Brissot, a man afterwards but too famous; an anec-
dote which proves how early this aversion had taken place. In
a conversation which, shortly before the breaking out of the
French revolution, he had with Mr. John Adams, now President of the United States, this gentleman assured him he was
firmly convinced, that France, by the approaching revolution,
would not even attain the degree of political liberty enjoyed
by England; and what is most important, he denied, in perfect consistency with his pure and rigorous principles, that the
French had a *right* to affect such a revolution as they intended.
Brissot attempted in vain by appeals to the *original compact,* to
the imprescriptibility of the rights of the people, and the like
revolutionary rant, to combat him.—P. Nouveau Voyage dans
les Etats Unis de l'Amérique, par Brissot. Vol. I. p. 147.[41]

When Paine's work appeared, in the year 1776, the American revolution had long since assumed its whole form and consistence, and the principles, which will forever characterize it stood firm. In no public resolve, in no public debate, in no state paper of congress, is the most distant expression to be found, which discovers either a formal, or a tacit approbation of a systematical revolutionary policy. And what a contrast between the wild, extravagant, rhapsodical declamation of a Paine, and the mild, moderate, and considerate tone in the speeches and letters of a Washington.[43]

The preciseness of objects, the uniformity of means, and the moderation of principles, which distinguished the American revolution through all its periods, gave likewise to the war, which was carried on for its establishment and completion, a precise and definite, and, therefore, a less formidable character. With this war indeed, the whole train of evils, which usually attend upon war in general, and especially upon civil war, were connected. But as it had only one object, and that was clearly known, and confined within narrow bounds, its possible results, its possible consequences, and its possible duration, could in every case be calculated. America had either to maintain or to give up her independence; in this single alternative was included the whole fate of the contest; and whatever consequence either event might operate upon a distant futurity, neither the victory of the British parliament, nor that (which very early became more probable) of the American congress, could discompose the balance of Europe, or threaten its peace. The governments of our hemisphere could, with all the tranquillity of a perfect neutrality, look forward to the issue of a remote contest, which, without further danger to their external and internal political relations, opened an advantageous prospect to the European commerce. The congress might even form an alliance with one of the greatest European monarchies; for as they only wished to maintain clear and definite rights, as they owed their existence to a revolution, which was forced upon the colonies by external violence, as they had at no time, and in no way, so much as called in question, much less attacked, the lawfulness of other constitutions, and as they had declared war, not against monarchical principles, but only against the oppressive measures of the British ministry, there was, *in itself,* nothing unnatural, nothing revolting, nothing plainly irreconcileable with the maxims of the law of nations, and the laws of self-preservation, in the alliance, which France contracted with them.*[44]

* I purposely say, there was nothing of *itself* illegal in this alliance. For France found the independence of the colonies already founded, when she contracted an alliance with them, and might besides not shrink from the question as to the lawfulness of this independence. Nothing *of itself,* unnatural, or self destructive; for the principles of the Americans contained immediately nothing, which could in any manner be dangerous to the existence of the French monarchy: and the political and commercial interests of this monarchy seemed in a manner to force its taking a part in the American revolution.

All this however notwithstanding, I believe, with the most

The peace, which concluded the American war, secured that existence independent of England, to the new federal republic, for which she had alone and

---

intimate conviction, that a more profound policy than that of the count de Vergennes,[45] and a larger and more comprehensive view into futurity, would have prevented France from contracting that alliance. Not to mention the false calculation which burdened with a new debt of one thousand millions of livres, a state already very much disordered in its finances, in order to do its rival, in the most favourable contingency, an uncertain damage. The whole undertaking was resolved on without any real political regard to its remote consequences. The lawfulness of the American revolution, might be ever so clearly demonstrated to a man capable of judging of its origin, and of appreciating the grounds upon which it was supported; the time might come, when without regard to the particular situation of the colonies, the general indefinite principle of insurrection might be taken alone, from their revolution, and applied to justify the most dangerous crimes. The Americans might ever so cautiously keep within their rigorous limits; and neither maintain, nor care for the application of their principles to other states; at the first great commotion, those whom the French cabinet had sent into the republican school, might with the forms consecrated in America, put all the European governments to the ban, and declare lawful and even virtuous *under all circumstances*, what had been allowable only *under certain circumstances*. These possible consequences of the co-operation of France would not have escaped the penetration of a truly great statesman, and the world has paid dearly enough for their having been overlooked.

exclusively contended, and immediately after, this republic entered into those peaceable and beneficent
relations with all other states, and even with England
herself, which the common wants, and the common
laws of nations have founded between civilized states.
It is true; the American revolution had in latter times
a decisive influence upon the great devastations under
which Europe groans to this hour;[46] but it would be
the highest injustice not to acknowledge that this influence was only accidental. In the origin of that revolution there was nothing that could justify another, or
even revolutions in general; no state, other than one,
in which all the extraordinary circumstances concurring in the case of the colonies, should again concur,
could consider the conduct observed by these, as le-
gitimating a similar conduct, and adopt the principles
upon which they proceeded. The precision and lawfulness of their object refused every application of these
principles to revolutions, which could not exhibit an
object equally definite, and a right equally clear, to the
pursuit of that object. The wise moderation, which the
leaders of the American revolution introduced into
all their declarations, and into every step they took,
their glorious abhorrence of every extravagance, even
of those proceeding from the most pardonable enthusiasm, the constant distance at which they kept
from every thing that may be called proselyting and
propagandism—all these happy characteristics of
their undertaking must in a legal point of view forever secure humanity against all evil consequences of

this revolution; whose only traces remaining, should be in the growing prosperity of a great people, spread over extensive and fertile regions, and above all in the wholesome lesson it gave to the powers of the earth against every attack upon the rights and constitutions of states, from ambition, or a spirit of innovation. The harshest injustice alone could impute to the Americans, what the ill-understood and misused example of their revolution has produced of evil in latter times; it was the work of an hostile demon, who seems to have condemned the close of the eighteenth century, to see the buds of destruction shoot from the most beneficent events, and the most poisonous fruits from the blossoms of its fairest hopes.[47]

The contrast between the French and American revolutions, when you compare them with each other in respect to their *objects* is no less striking than that which has resulted from the comparison of their *origin* and *progress*. As the utmost precision of object, and consequently of principles and of means, distinguished the American revolution through its whole duration, so the utmost want of precision in the object, and consequently a perpetual mutability in the choice of the means and in the modification of principles has been one of the most stubborn, one of the most essential, and certainly one of the most terrible characteristics of the French revolution. Its history was nothing but a long series of uninterrupted developments of this extraordinary phenomenon; single and unexampled in its whole compass as this circumstance may be, it will not much astonish the man, who shall reflect upon its origin, and its nature. For so soon as in a great undertaking, a step is taken wholly out of the boundaries of definite rights, and every thing is declared lawful, which imaginary necessity, or unbridled passion inspires, so soon is the immeasurable field of arbitrary will entered upon; and a revolution, which has no other principle than to attack the existing constitution, must necessarily proceed to the last extremities of imagination and of criminal guilt.

When, by the impotence and the faults of the government, and by the success which crowned the hardiness of its first antagonists, the old constitution of France was dissolved, all those who took an interest in favour of the revolution (and their number was infinitely great, precisely because no one knew exactly what he meant by a revolution) concurred, that an essential and wide spreading alteration must be effected in the whole political constitution of the state. But how far this alteration should extend, how far the old order of things should be preserved, and how the new one should be organized, with regard to all this, no two persons of the legions, who thought themselves called to public activity, were agreed. If we confine ourselves merely to the opinions of those, who in this interval of unbounded anarchy, publicly wrote, or spoke, we shall soon be convinced, that there were then in France, not three, or four, or ten, but thousands of political sects and parties. The impossibility of taking notice of so many individual variations, distinctions, sub-distinctions, and shades of every kind, compelled the contemporaries, and especially those immediately interested in the great spectacle, to class the infinite mass of opinions under certain known principal titles, and thus erase the names of *pure royalists,* of whole and half *monarchists,* of *feuillants,*[48] of *jacobins,*[49] of every degree, &c. Each of these parties, however, could have exhibited almost as many subordinate parties as it contained members.

In this number of political systems, some were built upon a limited monarchy, in the British sense of the word, others upon a thousand-fold new modification of a constitution, monarchical only in name; some wished from the beginning, to treat the revolution merely as a passage to the utter abolition of the monarchy. These pronounced sentence of death upon all the privileges of the higher orders; others wished to leave them the prerogatives of rank. One was for reforming the constitution of the churches; another for extirpating religion: one would have shewn mercy in this general overthrow, at least to the rights of property; another was for passing all positive right, under the sickle of equality. The constitution of 1791, was a desperate and impotent attempt to reconcile together, by a sort of general capitulation, all these contending theories, and the infinitely multiplied motives of interest, of ambition, and of vanity, connected with them; this attempt of course failed, for in the absolute and total indefiniteness, and I might add, the impossibility of ascertaining the last object of the revolution, every individual in France felt but too well, that he had as much right to maintain his private opinion, and to carry through his private purposes, as the members of a committee had to establish theirs; it was, besides, more than doubtful, whether, even the immediate authors of this impracticable constitution, seriously considered it as a last result.

Under the shelter of the inexpressible confusion, in which the storm of these first debates involved the whole country, arose, at first, more timid, but from the last months of the year 1791, growing constantly bolder, and more powerful, the only consistent party; that which had always been of opinion, that it was folly to prescribe to the French revolution, any bounds whatsoever. This party had, indeed, like all the rest, a multitude of subdivisions, and of systems peculiarly modified, and often at violent strife with each other; but all who declared themselves for it, concurred in the great and decisive point of view, that the revolution was to be considered, not as a local transaction, but as one of those, which give a new form to civil society, and which must draw all mankind within its vortex. For the ambition, or for the enthusiasm of this insatiable party, the theatre, which France offered to their thirst for destruction, was too small; they wished to tear up the world from its poles, and commence a new æra for the whole human race.[50] That this was their purpose, from the very breaking out, and even before the breaking out of the French revolution, we need not learn from proselyting tales and imaginary cabals of the illuminati; the writings in which they have unfolded their principles in plain terms, have proved it beyond all contradiction.

To draw nearer the execution of so gigantic a plan, they had first of all to destroy the last trace of a monarchical form of government in France. It would be hard to maintain, that, after all what had happened since 1789, they had not nearly about the same right to found a republic, as the monarchists, so called, had to introduce a royal democracy. The only thing which seemed against them, in point of right, was the oath which, in common with all the rest, they had taken, to support the constitution of 1791. But, after so many bands had been torn, none but weak heads could flatter themselves, that an empty form would arrest the torrent in its course. At the very time, while, with the cry of "The constitution or death!" they hushed a few credulous souls to repose, they were working with restless activity the mine, which in one instant was to blow up the whole fabric.

But, precisely at this great and important moment, the absolute indefinitude of object, that inextinguishable character of the French revolution, discovered itself in a new and terrible light. The republic had been proclaimed;[51] but this republic was a word without definite meaning, which every one believed he might explain, according to his inclinations, and according to the fantastic whims, which he called his principles. There were just as many republican systems contending for the mastery, as there had been monarchical parties. France was drenched in blood, to decide the great question, whether Brissot, or Marat, the federalists, or the unitists, the Girondists, or the mountain-

eers, the Dantonians, or the Hebertists, should prescribe a republican constitution.[52] Force alone could
determine the issue of this horrible contest; and the
victory must necessarily remain to the most resolute.
After having torn, for nearly a year, the inmost bowels
of their country, without being able to agree upon the
form of their republic, a daring faction, at length, fell
upon the strange expedient of settling and organizing
the revolutionary state itself, as a provisional government, and, under the name of a revolutionary government, brought into play what was called the system
of terror;[53] a monstrous and unexampled monument
of human error and human frenzy, which in the eyes of
posterity will almost degrade the history of our times
to a fable. A less cruel faction overthrew and murdered
the inventors of this gigantic wickedness; not long
afterwards, another devised a new code of anarchy,
which was called the constitution of the third year.[54]
It is well known, by what an uninterrupted series of
revolutions, and counter-revolutions, this constitution
was likewise conducted to the unavoidable catastrophe
of its destruction.

Just at the period, when the republican party obtained possession of the supreme power, the bloody
contest broke out between them and the greatest part
of the European states.[55] They had denounced the destruction of all governments; they had declared, that
between their revolution and those who rejected it,
no further intercourse could exist; they had solemnly
absolved all subjects from obedience to their govern-

ments.[56] The revolution prepared against Europe, and Europe against the revolution, a war, with which only the most dreadful religious wars, that ever scourged the world, can be compared.[57] On the side of the co-alesced powers, the proper object of this war could not be doubtful; and if, unfortunately, it often was, at least it ought never to have been so. But, on the side of France, it was always as indefinite as the object of the revolution itself. Some, as for instance, Robespierre, wished for the present, only to maintain the right of turning their own country into a butchery, with im-punity, and to reduce by one half the number of its inhabitants; others had projected extensive plans of conquest, and wished to realize for the French repub-lic, all the dreams, which the ambition of Lewis the XIVth,[58] had formerly inspired; others yet had sworn never to lay down their arms, until they should have led the principles of the revolution in triumph over the whole civilized world, or *have planted, at least,* the tree of liberty, from Lisbon to the frozen sea, and to the Dardanelles.

This war has now, with short and local intervals of insecure and treacherous peace, already desolated the earth eight years long; it has, undoubtedly, for some time past, lost much of its extent, and very much of its original character, and has now nearly declined to a common war; yet when and how it will end, is still a problem, which puts all human penetration to the blush. The fate of the French revolution is, in a great measure, connected with the fate of this war; but its last result depends, besides, upon an infinity of other combinations. There has, perhaps, never yet been a man, who could even imagine, with any clearness, what this result will be. When one of the great masses of the physical world is suddenly started from its quiet centre of gravitation, and hurled with a prodigious impetus into the empty space of air, the point at which it will stop is much harder to conceive, than the continuance of its motion. And, in truth, after the serious question, Who could have a right to begin such a revolution? has remained unanswered, nothing is more difficult than to answer that, which is equally serious: to whom belongs the right of ending it?

4. The American revolution had a mass of resistance, comparatively much smaller to combat, and, therefore, could form and consolidate itself in a manner comparatively much easier, and more simple: the French revolution challenged almost every human feeling, and every human passion, to the most vehement resistance, and could therefore only force its way by violence and crimes.

The American colonies had already, before their revolution, attained a high degree of stability; and the supremacy of the British government in America, was the relation, not so much of an immediate sovereign, as of a superior protector. Hence, the American revolution had more the appearance of a foreign, than of a civil war.

A common feeling of the uprightness of their cause, and a common interest in its issue must necessarily have animated a great and overpowering majority of the inhabitants of North America. The royal governors, the persons more immediately connected with them, and the inconsiderable number of royal troops constituted the only permanent and great opposition party. If a certain number of independent citizens, from principle, or from inclination took the side of the ministry, they were however much too weak to become dangerous to the rest; and their impotence itself protected them against the hatred and intolerance of their countrymen.

There were in the interior of the colonies no sort of zeal or personal prerogatives, and no other distinction of ranks, than what proceeded from the exercise of public functions. Property owing to the novelty of civil society in the country, was much more equally distributed than can be the case in old countries, and the relations between the wealthy and the labouring classes were more simple and therefore more beneficent. As the revolution altered little in the internal organization of the colonies, as it only dissolved an external connection, which the Americans must always have considered rather as a burden, than an advantage; there was nobody, except the few, who took a share in the administration at the head of the country, who was immediately and essentially interested in the preservation of the ancient form. What this form contained of good and useful remained untouched; the revolution only removed that in which it had been oppressive.

How infinitely different was in this point of view

the situation of France! If the French revolution had
been content merely to destroy with violent hands the
old Constitution, without making any attack upon the
rights and possessions of private persons,[59] it would,
however, have been contrary to the interest of a numerous, and in every respect important class of people,
who by the sudden dissolution of the old form of Government, having lost their offices, their incomes, their
estimation and their whole civil existence, would of
themselves have formed a powerful opposition—But,
when in its further progress, it no longer spared any
private right whatsoever, when it declared all political
prerogatives to be usurpations, deprived the nobility
not only of their real privileges, but likewise of their
rank and title, robbed the clergy of their possessions,
of their influence, and even of their external dignity;
by arbitrary laws took from the holders of estates half
their revenues; by incessant breaches of the rights of
property, converted property itself into an uncertain,
equivocal, narrowly straitened enjoyment, by recog-
nizing publicly principles of the most dangerous tendency, held the sword hovering over the head of every
one, who had any thing to lose, and aggravated the
essential wretchedness, which it every where spread
by the ridicule and contempt it shed over every thing
that bore the name of possessions, or priviledges—
then truly it could not fail to accumulate against itself
a mass of resistance, which was not to be subdued by
ordinary means.

Should the friends of the French revolution declare

this important circumstance to be merely accidental; should they impute solely to the good fortune of the American nation, that they found no domestic impediments in the way to their new constitution; and to the ill fortune of the French, that they had to struggle with so many obstinate antagonists; should they consider the former case only as enviable, and the latter only as deserving compassion, yet will the impartial observer, never forget how much merit there was involved in that good, and how much guilt in this ill fortune. The Americans were wise enough to circumscribe themselves within the bounds, which right, on one side, and the nature of things, on the other, had drawn round them. The French in their giddiness no longer acknowledged the prescriptions of the clearest right, nor the prescriptions of nature. They were so proud as to think they could bend impossibility itself, under the arm of their violence,[60] and so daring that they thought the clearest right must yield to the maxims of their arbitrary will. The resistance of which they complained, was with perfect certainty to be foreseen; it lay in the unalterable laws of human feelings, and human passions; it was just, it was necessary; it was impossible to believe that it would not take place. Those, who had called it forth by the most cruel injuries, did not fail to be sure to declare it punishable, and did punish thousands, whose only crime consisted in refusing to rejoice at their own ruin. But this double injustice prepared a new resistance, which could be overcome only by new acts of violence. Thus at last, in the barbarous

law book of the revolution, suffering itself was made
an unpardonable offence; the fear of a just reaction
drove the authors of these oppressions to measures of
still deepening cruelty against the victims of their first
crimes; and the presumption of the natural and inevitable hatred, which these crimes must every where
rouse against them, was a sufficient ground to them to
treat as an offender deserving death, every man, who
did not immediately and actively associate with them.

Although the American revolution never involved
itself in this horrible labyrinth, where voluntary iniq-
uities can only be covered by necessary misdeeds, and
where every earlier crime became the only justification
of an hundred later ones; yet did it not altogether escape the misfortune, which seems inseparable from all
sudden and violent changes in the civil and political
relations of society. The smallness of the resistance it
met with, and the moderation of those who conducted
it, preserved it from a multitude of cruel, desperate,
and dishonorable measures, which have sullied other
revolutions; but its warmest friends will not venture to
maintain that it was wholly exempt from injustice and
violence. The bitterness against the English government, often degenerated into a spirit of persecution,
and involved those, who were suspected of a punishable indifference, or of secret connivance, in the sentence of proscription pronounced against tyranny. The
hatred between the friends of independence, and the
partizans of the ministry, the whigs and the tories,[61] as
they were distinguished by names taken from old En-

glish parties, broke out, especially amidst the dangers of the war, sometimes in violent scenes, which tore to pieces the internal harmony of neighbourhoods, and sometimes even of families. The reciprocal cruelties, which from time to time were practised upon prisoners, called to mind the peculiar character, which had never wholly abandoned a civil war. The rights of property likewise were often violated by single communities and single states, and, in some few instances, with the co-operation of the supreme authority. The history of the descendents, of the great and benevolent Penn, driven from the paradise, which he had created, and compelled, like other loyalists, to take refuge in the generosity and magnanimity of England, is no honorable page in the annals of North-America.

But what are all these single instances of injustice and oppression, compared with the universal flood of misery and ruin, which the French revolution let loose upon France, and all the neighbouring countries. If, even in America, private hatred, or local circumstances, threatened property or personal security; if here and there even the public authorities became the instruments of injustice, of revenge, and of a persecuting spirit, yet did the poison never flow into every vein of the social body; never, as in France, was the contempt of all rights, and of the very simplest precepts of humanity, made the general maxim of legislation, and the unqualified prescription of systematic tyranny. If in America, the confusion of the moment, the impulse of necessity, or the eruption of the passions, sometimes inflicted misfortune upon innocence, never at least, never as in France, did reason herself, abused, desecrated reason, ascend the theatre of misery, solemnly to justify, by cold blooded, criminal appeals to principles and duties, these revolutionary confusions; and if in America, single families and districts, felt the heavy hand of the revolution and of war, never at least, as in France, were confiscations, banishments, imprisonments, and death, decreed in a mass.

When the American revolution was concluded, the country proceeded with rapid steps to a new, a happy, and a flourishing constitution. Not but that the revolution had left behind it many great and essential ravages: the ties of public order, had, in a long and bloody contest, been on all sides more or less relaxed; peaceful industry had suffered many a violent interruption; the relations of property, the culture of the soil, the internal and foreign trade, the public and private credit, had all considerably suffered by the revolutionary storms, by the insecurity of the external relations, and especially by the devastations of paper money.* Even the morals

---

* In no one point is the analogy between the conduct of the revolutionary leaders in America and in France, so striking as in this; yet it must not be forgotten, that the Americans failed partly from inexperience and partly from real necessity; whereas in France they knew very well what they were about, and opened and widened the precipice with design.

The history of the American assignats,[62] is almost word for word, only upon a smaller scale, and not attended with circum-

and the character of the people, had been essentially, and not in every respect advantageously affected by the revolution. Although we can draw no conclusion from this circumstance with regard to futurity, yet history must remark with attention, and preserve with care, the confession, which comes from the pen of a calm and impartial witness, the best of all the writers upon the American revolution hitherto (Ramsay):[63] "That by

---

stances of such shocking cruelty, as the history of the French ones. The sudden start from two millions to two hundred millions of dollars; the credulity with which the first assignats were received, the undeserved credit which they for a time enjoyed, their subsequent rapid fall, so that in the year 1777, they already stood with specie in the proportion of 1 to 3; in 1778, of 1 to 6; in 1779, of 1 to 28; in the beginning of 1780, of 1 to 60; fell immediately afterwards to that of 1 to 150, and finally would pass for nothing at all; the attempt to substitute a new emission of assignats, instead of those which were worn out, continued until at last it became necessary to establish a formal depreciation; the harsh laws made to support the value of the paper; the regulation of the price of provisions (the maximum) and the requisitions, which they occasioned; the general devastation of property, and disturbance of all civil intercourse; the wretchedness and immorality which ensued upon them—all this goes to compose a picture, which the French revolutionary leaders seem to have taken for a model. It is remarkable, that they closely copied the Americans only in two points, of which one was the idlest, and the other the most objectionable of any throughout their revolution; in the declaration of the rights of man, and in paper-money.

this revolution, the *political, military,* and *literary* talents of the people of the United States, were improved, but their *moral* qualities were deteriorated."

A picture of the condition in which the revolution has left France, is by far too great, too complicated, and too formidable a subject to be touched upon even transiently here. The idea itself of a final result from such a revolution as this, must still be in some sort an indefinite, and perhaps a hazarded idea. Thus much, however, may be asserted with confidence, that between the results of the American and those of the French revolution, no sort of comparison can so much as be conceived.

I might have continued the above parallel through many other respects, and perhaps into single points of detail. I believe, however, that the four principal points of view in which I have treated it, with regard to the *lawfulness of the origin, character of the conduct, quality of the object,* and *compass of resistance,* sufficiently answer the purpose, I proposed to myself, and it appears, at least to me, evident enough, that every parallel between these two revolutions, will serve much more to display the *contrast,* than the *resemblance* between them.

THE END

Editor's Notes

Introduction

1. Eugen Rosenstock-Huessy, *Out of Revolution: Autobiography of Western Man* (Providence and Oxford: Berg Publishers, 1993). German original: *Die Europäischen Revolutionen und der Charakter der Nationen* (1931) (Stuttgart: W. Kohlhammer, 3rd ed., 1961).

Preface

1. It is a rare, if not a unique, event that a book by a European author is translated by a man of erudition who will later become the president of the United States of America. John Quincy Adams, the sixth president of the United States, from March 4, 1825 to March 4, 1829, had met Gentz in Berlin around the year 1800 while he was ambassador of the United States of America to Prussia. George Washington appointed Adams minister to the Netherlands (at the age of twenty-six)

in 1794 and to Portugal in 1796. Adams then was promoted to the Berlin Legation. When John Adams became president, he appointed his son in 1797 as minister to Prussia at Washington's urging. There Adams signed the renewal of the very liberal Prussian-American Treaty of Amity and Commerce, after negotiations with Prussian foreign minister Count Karl-Wilhelm Finck von Finckenstein. He served at that post until 1801.

Adams's respect for Gentz and his judgment about the importance of Gentz's text are confirmed by a letter to Gentz preceding the translation. The letter is reproduced here in full. (John Quincy Adams, "Letter to Friedrich Gentz dated Berlin, June 16, 1800," in *The Writings of John Quincy Adams*, ed. Worthington Chauncey Ford [New York: Macmillan, 1913], vol. 2, 1796–1801, 463–64.)

"SIR:

I had already perused with great pleasure the comparison between the origin and principles of the French and American revolutions contained in the *Historical Journal* for the two last months, before receiving the copies which you had the goodness to send me yesterday. It cannot but afford a gratification to every American attached to the honor of his country to see its revolution so ably vindicated from the imputation of having originated, or been conducted upon the same principles as that of France, and I feel myself as an American Citizen highly obliged to you for the consideration you have bestowed upon the subject, as well as for the honorable manner in which you have borne testimony to the purity of principle upon which the revolution of my country was founded. I beg you, sir, to accept my best thanks for your very acceptable present and to be assured that I shall take much satisfaction in transmitting and making known the treatise to persons in the United States capable of estimating its merits."

Adams's letter to Gentz is from June 1800. In that same year, his translation was published in Philadelphia. Adams must have produced and finished the translation at great speed during the summer of 1800. To his brother Thomas Boylston Adams, Adams writes about the translation:

"MY DEAR BROTHER:

The translation of Gentz's essay is published with a neatness and accuracy with which I ought to be more than satisfied. The type and paper are such as we can present without blushing to any foreigner's eye. The only circumstance of regret to me was that by your absence at the time of publication you were prevented from expunging those Germanisms, and other blunders of uncorrected taste, which a number of circumstances that I will not now trouble you with had prevented me from removing. All the passages which you had marked on the corrected copy and many others, I altered myself in a copy which I sent to England with view of having it published there." (John Quincy Adams, "Letter to Thomas Boylston Adams, Dated Berlin, 21 March, 1801," in *The Writings of John Quincy Adams,* loc. cit., 520.)

2. To Adams's regret, the English booksellers did not find the book so interesting for an English public, which comes as no surprise, since nations do not like to be reminded of their defeats. The first American reactions, however, proved to be favorable. The quotation of Adams's letter to his brother continues:

"But the booksellers, though of opinion that it was a work of *considerable merit,* thought the subject not sufficiently *interest-*

ing to please an English public. There are, indeed, obvious reasons why the language and sentiments of that pamphlet should not be very interesting to English ears, and I could not blame the discretion of the booksellers, though somewhat diverted with the ingenuity of their objection against the publication. I learn with pleasure from you that the opinions you have heard expressed of it are uniformly favorable. The merit of the translation is nothing, or worse than nothing. *Drudgery* at most, which it is usual to despise, even when we commend it. But the merit of the original author is so well known and so firmly established in every part of Europe, that if in our country too the pamphlet should not prove sufficiently interesting to reward a bookseller for printing it, I shall not only despair of the taste, but of the patriotism of our fellow citizens. [. . .] For the honor of our country, therefore, I hope that your friend the bookseller will have no occasion to repent his share in the publication of the essay." (Ibid., 520–21.)

Text

1. The American Revolution describes the political process during the last half of the eighteenth century in which the thirteen colonies among the possessions in North America of the Kingdom of Great Britain became the sovereign United States of America. They first rejected the governance of the Parliament of Great Britain, and later the British monarchy itself. The colonies expelled all royal officials and, by 1774, set up thirteen Provincial Congresses or equivalent assemblies to form individual self-governing states. Through representatives sent in 1775 to the Second Continental Congress, they

united to defend their respective self-governance and fought the armed conflict against the British known as the American Revolutionary War (1775–83, also American War of Independence). The states collectively made the decision that the British monarchy, by acts of tyranny, could no longer legitimately claim their allegiance. They united to form one nation, completing the break away from the British Empire in July 1776 when the Congress issued the Declaration of Independence, rejecting the monarchy on behalf of the United States of America. The war ended with effective American victory in October 1781. Britain abandoned any claims to the United States with the Treaty of Paris in 1783. The basic rules of national governance were settled with the unanimous ratification in 1788 of the Constitution of the United States (written in 1787). The American Constitution, therefore, completed the process of American independence or the American Revolution one year before the French Revolution started in 1789. The end of the American Revolution thus almost coincides with the beginning of the French Revolution.

2. Among the main French personages who had been active in the American and French revolutions is Marie-Joseph Paul Yves Roch Gilbert du Motier, Marquis de La Fayette (or Lafayette, 1757–1834), a French aristocrat and military officer. Lafayette was a general in the American Revolutionary War and a leader of the National Guard (*Garde Nationale*) during the French Revolution. For his contributions to the American Revolution, many cities and monuments throughout the United States bear his name, such as Fayetteville, North Carolina, the only town bearing his name that Lafayette actually visited in person. He was the first person granted honorary U.S. citizenship. During France's July Revolution of

1830, in the period after Napoleon, Lafayette declined an offer to become the French dictator; instead he supported Louis-Philippe's bid as a constitutional monarch.

Several representatives of the French National Constituent Assembly (*l'Assemblée Constituante*) had participated in the American Revolution, like Lafayette, or admired it deeply, like Condorcet. Marie Jean Antoine Nicolas de Caritat, Marquis de Condorcet (1743–94), known as Nicolas de Condorcet, was a French philosopher, mathematician, and early political scientist and politician who belonged to the liberal faction of the French Revolution.

The Virginia Declaration of Rights of 1776 inspired the French Declaration of the Human and Civic Rights (*Déclaration des Droits de l'Homme et du Citoyen* of August 1789). In November 1788 Lafayette edited a project of the Declaration of Rights for France, asking Thomas Jefferson for advice.

On the American side, two of the founding fathers of the United States of America must be named. The first is Benjamin Franklin (1706–90), who had been active in the American Revolution and exerted influence in France in the years before the French Revolution. As a diplomat during the American Revolution and as ambassador to France in the years 1776 to 1785, he secured the French alliance that helped to achieve the independence of the United States. He conducted the affairs of the United States vis-à-vis the French nation with great success by securing a critical military alliance in 1778, and he negotiated the Treaty of Paris in 1783. When he finally returned home in 1785, Franklin occupied a position second only to that of George Washington as the champion of American independence. He is the only founding father who was a signatory of all four of the major documents of the founding of the United States: the Declaration of Independence, the

Treaty of Paris, the Treaty of Alliance with France, and the U.S. Constitution.

The other prominent founding father who supported both revolutions is Thomas Jefferson, third president of the United States. Jefferson was United States minister (ambassador) to France in the years 1785 to 1789. He left Paris in September 1789, shortly after the outbreak of the French Revolution. Jefferson had taken sides with the revolutionaries as far as his diplomatic post allowed him to do so.

3. There is also the historical commonplace of the "Atlantic Revolutions," which tends to put all revolutions in the countries around the Northern Atlantic into the one category of "Atlantic Revolution."

4. Gentz refers to the Jacobin Reign of Terror in the years after the beginning of the French Revolution in July 1789.

5. Gentz ascribes the salutary consequences to the American Revolution and cautions the reader not to ascribe the unhealthy consequences of the French Revolution only to misfortune and unfortunate circumstances.

6. Adam Smith made the suggestion to give representation to the North American colonies in the British Parliament. He even predicted without resentment that the capital of the British Empire would eventually be moved to America. (The American Revolution had already started when Smith wrote his book.) See Adam Smith, *The Wealth of Nations* (1776), ed. R. H. Campbell, A. S. Skinner, and W. B. Todd (Oxford: Clarendon Press, 1976), IV., VII. c. 74, 621–22.

Josiah Tucker (1713–99), also known as Dean Tucker, an economist and political writer, published *A Brief Essay on the Advantages and Disadvantages, which Respectively Attend France and Great Britain* (1749). Tucker argued with both Edmund Burke and John Wilkes about the politics toward Britain's American colonies and took a particular position on the American War of Independence. As early as 1766, he considered the separation to be inevitable. He was, however, also hostile to the Americans. He wrote several pamphlets, including *A Series of Answers to Certain Popular Objections against Separating from the Rebellious Colonies* (1776).

7. In contrast to the Spanish colonies in South America, according to Gentz, the North American colonies and the United States are important not because gold and silver can be extracted from them but because they form a new huge single market for their own and for European wares. This argument was previously developed by Gentz in his essay of 1795, *Ueber den Einfluß der Entdeckung von Amerika auf den Wohlstand und die Cultur des menschlichen Geschlechts* (On the Influence of the Discovery of America on the Wealth and the Civilization of the Human Race), first published in *Neue Deutsche Monatsschrift*, August 1795, 269–319; reprinted in Friedrich Gentz, *Gesammelte Schriften* (Collected Works), ed. Günther Kronenbitter (Hildesheim, Zürich, New York: Olms-Weidmann, 1998), vol. 7, *Kleine Schriften*, 168–217.

8. What Gentz refers to is the Seven Years' War, 1756 to 1763, known as the French and Indian War in North America. This war is considered by some to be the first "world war," or war fought on different continents. It was fought between the European powers over territorial gains in the colonies and predominance in Europe. The war ended with the Treaty of Paris in 1763. In 1762, a separate, secret peace treaty had been concluded between Britain, France, and Spain about the North American territories in Louisiana, Florida, and Canada. This treaty, the Treaty of Fontainebleau (a town near Paris) of 1762, had been kept secret, even at the Treaty of Paris, until 1764. It makes sense, however, to consider the Treaty of

Fontainebleau to be part of the Seven Years' War, in which, among others, Prussia attained her new status as a European great power by seizing the province of Silesia (now mainly in Poland) from Austria.

9. Gentz emphasizes the link between the impulse to have political control over a colony and the wish to control its market, thereby giving the motherland a monopoly of trade over the colony.

10. Gentz points out that levying an American public tax the revenue from which was to be used in Britain is one more aspect of a policy that restricted American trade with Britain so as to favor British wares in North America. Above, on p. 19, Gentz compares the trade monopoly of Britain in the colonies to a tax levied on the North American colonies. See also above, p. 60, where Gentz quotes the Second Continental Congress of the United States, calling the British monopoly of trade with the colonies "the heaviest of all contributions."

11. *Specie* means "hard" currency: gold and silver.

12. George Grenville (1712–70) was a British Whig statesman who served in government for the relatively short period of seven years. In April 1763, he became first lord of the treasury and chancellor of the exchequer. He was prime minister of Great Britain from April 16, 1763 to July 13, 1765, during which time he was confronted with the growing discontent in British America that led to open rebellion.

13. *Colonial immunity* means here colonial exception from being taxed for the expenditures of the motherland.

14. The marquess of Rockingham was a man of great talents. When in Herrenhausen, Hanover, Germany (then united with Great Britain in personal union, since the king of Great Britain was also king of Hanover), Rockingham met King George II and made an excellent impression: the king told

Rockingham's uncle, Henry Finch, that he had never seen a finer or a more promising youth.

15. William Pitt, first earl of Chatham (1708–78), was a British Whig statesman who achieved his greatest fame leading Britain during the Seven Years' War. He again led the country (holding the official title of Lord Privy Seal) between 1766 and 1768. He is often known as William Pitt the Elder, to distinguish him from his son, William Pitt the Younger. He was also known as the Great Commoner, because of his long-standing refusal to accept a title of nobility, until 1766. Pittsburgh, Pennsylvania, is named after him, as are numerous other cities and towns in the United States, Canada, and Australia.

16. Frederick North, second earl of Guilford (1732–92), more often known by his courtesy title, Lord North, which he used from 1752 until 1790, was prime minister of Great Britain from 1770 to 1782. He led Great Britain through most of the American War of Independence. He also held a number of other cabinet posts, including home secretary and chancellor of the exchequer.

17. The East India Company, also known as the East India Trading Company, the English East India Company, and then the British East India Company, was an early English joint-stock company. It was formed initially for pursuing trade with the East Indies but traded in fact mainly with the Indian subcontinent and China.

18. Edmund Burke (1729–97) was an Anglo-Irish statesman, author, orator, political theorist, and philosopher who served for many years in the House of Commons of Great Britain as a member of the Whig party. He is remembered mainly for his opposition to the French Revolution. It led to his becoming the leading figure within the conservative faction of the Whig party, which he dubbed the "Old Whigs," in opposition to the

pro–French Revolution "New Whigs," led by Charles James Fox. Burke and William Pitt, Lord Chatham, were considered to be great parliamentary speakers. Burke's central work is *Considerations on the Revolution in France,* of 1790, one of the first critiques of the French Revolution by a political philosopher. Gentz translated it into German and published it in two parts, in 1793–94.

19. The Battles of Lexington and Concord were the first military engagements of the American Revolutionary War. They were fought on April 19, 1775, in Middlesex County, Province of Massachusetts Bay, within the towns of Lexington, Concord, Lincoln, Menotomy (present-day Arlington), and Cambridge, near Boston. The battles marked the outbreak of open armed conflict between the kingdom of Great Britain and its thirteen colonies in the mainland of British North America.

20. The letter became known as the Olive Branch petition. It was signed by forty-eight members of Congress and entrusted to Richard Penn of Pennsylvania, a descendant of William Penn, the founder of the colony. Gentz quotes this letter extensively above on pp. 61–62.

21. Historical theory contends that Britain turned to India after the loss of the American possessions. Since British forces were not needed in North America after American independence, Britain could concentrate on stabilizing its power in India. William Pitt the Younger and Richard Marquis Wellesley, general governor of the East India Company, 1797–1805, and British foreign minister, 1809–12, are said to have replaced North America with India for Britain. William Pitt the Younger (1759–1806) became the youngest prime minister of Britain in 1783, at the age of twenty-four. He left office in 1801, but was prime minister again from 1804 until his death, in 1806.

22. The right of revolution (*ius resistendi*, the right to resist

an unjust government, also right of resistance) has been discussed throughout history. On the eve of the American Revolution, Alexander Hamilton justified American resistance as an expression of "the law of nature" to fight violations of "the first principles of civil society" and invasions of "the rights of a whole people." (Alexander Hamilton, "The Farmer Refuted, [Feb. 23], 1775," in *The Papers of Alexander Hamilton*, ed. Harold C. Syrett and Jacob E. Cooke [New York: Columbia University Press, 1961], vol. 1, 136.) For Thomas Jefferson, the Declaration of Independence was the last possible recourse of an oppressed people—the position many Americans considered themselves in 1776 to be in. Jefferson's list of colonial grievances was the attempt to prove that the Americans were exercising nothing but the natural right of revolution. Usually, the right of revolution is not formulated as a positive right, although some states of the United States, such as Massachusetts, even inserted it into their constitution; rather, it was considered as part of natural right that overrules positive right if the government breaks its own laws or those of natural right. Critics of the right of revolution, such as Immanuel Kant, question the possibility of positive right to give a right not to follow its laws. Thomas Aquinas, although he affirms a right to resistance, and others point to the danger that tyrannical rule might be even worsened and become more oppressive if it must fear at all times a right of revolution. Gentz points to the difficulties, which require a very cautious treatment of the question whether there is a right to revolution in a given historical situation.

23. Gentz emphasizes that the constitutional development of Britain and her North American colonies did not happen at the same time. Sometimes the colonies lagged behind developments in Britain; sometimes some colonies led the de-

velopment toward constitutionalism. On the next page in the text, above, p. 40, Gentz emphasizes that the North American colonies were under the law of the crown and that there was no "trace of a constitutional and legal authority vested in the British parliament" over them. This fact made it even more difficult to judge which rights were held by the opposing sides, Britain and the colonies.

24. The Glorious Revolution, also called the Revolution of 1688, was the overthrow of King James II of England (VII of Scotland and II of Ireland) in 1688 by a union of parliamentarians with an invading army led by the Dutch stadtholder William III of Orange-Nassau (William of Orange). As a result, William ascended the English throne as William III of England. The Revolution of 1688 established the power of Parliament in Britain.

25. Whether these charters went so far as actually to grant the colonial assemblies the right of peace and war remains to be seen. In any case, it was the right of peace and war against external enemies, not against the British crown.

26. From the point of view of the colonies, the British parliament was not their parliament. It acted upon them as if it were a foreign power, a usurper. If the British king allied himself with the British parliament, he was acting like the ally of a foreign power toward the North American colonies. By this act of hostility toward the colonies he ceased to be their king, according to Gentz.

27. The real French Revolution started on July 14, 1789, with the storming of the Bastille, the state prison in Paris. It ended on November 9, 1799, or 18 Brumaire of the Year VIII, when Napoleon staged the coup of 18 Brumaire, which overthrew the Directory and installed the Consulate. This led to Bonaparte's dictatorship and eventually (in 1804) to his

proclamation as emperor, which put an end to the specifically republican phase of the French Revolution. (18 Brumaire of the Year VIII was part of the French Republican Calendar, or French Revolutionary Calendar.)

28. Louis XVI (1754–93) ruled as king of France and Navarre from 1774 until 1791, and then as king of the French from 1791 to 1792. Suspended and arrested during the insurrection of August 10, 1792, he was tried by the National Convention, found guilty of treason, and executed by guillotine on January 21, 1793. Louis XVI is seen by some historians as an honest man with good intentions but who was not able to fulfill the herculean task of reforming the monarchy. See also Gentz's characterization of the king above, pp. 63–64.

29. Gentz refers to the First Continental Congress, a convention of delegates from twelve of the thirteen North American colonies that met on September 5, 1774, at Carpenters' Hall in Philadelphia. Called in response to the passage of the Coercive Acts (also known as the Intolerable Acts in the American colonies) by the British parliament, the Congress was attended by fifty-six members appointed by the legislatures of twelve of the thirteen colonies, the exception being the Province of Georgia, which did not send delegates.

30. The Conciliatory Resolution was passed by the British parliament with the intention of reaching a peaceful settlement with the thirteen colonies immediately prior to the outbreak of the American Revolutionary War.

In January 1775, the British parliament considered petitions from the colonies in relation to the Coercive Acts, including a petition to the king from the First Continental Congress, and discussed ways to resolve the crisis with the thirteen colonies. A proposal by William Pitt to recognize colonial self-government was rejected by the House of Lords.

Pitt then moved for the withdrawal of troops from Boston, but that motion was defeated. In February, Pitt presented a plan of conciliation based upon mutual concessions, but this was also rejected. On February 2, despite fierce opposition from some members of Parliament, New England was declared to be in rebellion. Lord North took the unexpected role of conciliator for the drafting of a conciliatory resolution, which was passed on February 20, 1775 and dated February 27.

The Conciliatory Resolution declared that any colony that contributed to the common defense and provided support for the civil government and the administration of justice (ostensibly against any anti-Crown rebellion) would be relieved of paying taxes or duties except those necessary for the regulation of commerce.

The resolution was addressed and sent to the individual colonies, intentionally ignoring the extralegal Continental Congress. By doing this, Lord North hoped to divide the colonists among themselves and thus weaken any revolutionary independence movements, such as especially those represented by the Continental Congress. The resolution proved to be too little, too late, and the American Revolutionary War began at Lexington on April 19, 1775.

31. The Second Continental Congress was a convention of delegates from the thirteen colonies that met beginning on May 10, 1775, in Philadelphia, soon after warfare in the American Revolutionary War had begun. The second Congress coordinated the colonial war effort. It took measures toward independence and adopted the U.S. Declaration of Independence on July 2, 1776. The Congress acted as the de facto national government of what became the United States. Because of the ratification of the Articles of Confederation in 1781, this was later called the Congress of the Confederation.

32. W. Belsham, *Memoirs of the Reign of George III. to the Session of Parliament Ending A.D. 1793*, vol. 1 (London, 1796).

33. Louis XVI of France, see above, note 28.

34. *Civism* is archaic for "public spirit."

35. Maximilien François Marie Isidore de Robespierre (1758–94), one of the central figures of the French Revolution, dominated the Committee of Public Safety and led the period of the Revolution commonly known as the Reign of Terror, when the largest number of people was executed by the guillotine. The Terror ended with his arrest on July 27, 1794, and his execution the next day.

36. Gentz refers to David Ramsay, *The History of the American Revolution*, 1789. New edition with a foreword by Lester H. Cohen (Indianapolis: Liberty Fund, 1990), 2 vols.

37. Gentz considers the declaration of natural and unalienable rights of man as well as the idea of popular sovereignty as a superfluous rhetoric in the American Revolution and as a dangerous illusion and error in the French Revolution. Although the French Revolution, in the person of Lafayette, took over the ideas from the American Revolution, through Jefferson's advice to Lafayette, they were effective only in the French Revolution, producing, according to Gentz, serious error, political disaster, and human misery.

38. Thomas Paine (1737–1809), author, pamphleteer, revolutionary, inventor, and one of the founding fathers of the United States, also had great influence on the French Revolution. His principal contributions were the widely read pamphlet *Common Sense* (1776), advocating colonial America's independence from the kingdom of Great Britain, and the *Rights of Man* (1791), a guide to Enlightenment ideas. Although he did not speak French, he was elected to the French National Convention in 1792.

39. John Dickinson (1732–1808) was an American lawyer and politician from Philadelphia, Pennsylvania, and Wilmington, Delaware. He was successively a militia officer during the American Revolution, a Continental Congressman from Pennsylvania and Delaware, a delegate to the U.S. Constitutional Convention of 1787, president of Delaware, and president of Pennsylvania.

John Adams (1735–1826) was an American politician and the second president of the United States (1797–1801), after being the first vice president (1789–97) for two terms under George Washington. He is regarded as one of the most influential founding fathers. He was the father of John Quincy Adams, the translator of Gentz's text and later sixth president of the United States.

John Jay (1745–1829) was an American politician, statesman, revolutionary, diplomat, founding father, president of the Continental Congress from 1778 to 1779, and, from 1789 to 1795, the first chief justice of the United States. During and after the American Revolution, he was a minister (ambassador) to Spain and France, contributing to shaping U.S. foreign policy. He collaborated with Alexander Hamilton and James Madison on the serialized essays known as the *Federalist Papers*.

For Benjamin Franklin see above, note 2.

40. Richard Price (1723–91) was a British moral philosopher and preacher in the tradition of the English Dissenters, and a political pamphleteer, active in radical, republican, and liberal causes such as the American Revolution. He maintained relationships with many people, including writers of the Constitution of the United States. Richard Price supported the French Revolution. He gave an address before a meeting of the Revolution Society in London in favor of the new French National

Assembly. Immediately after reading a copy of Price's speech, Edmund Burke set about drafting his *Reflections on the Revolution in France*.

41. Jacques Pierre Brissot (1754–93), who assumed the name de Warville, was a leading member of the Girondist movement (see below note 52 for the different parties of the French Revolution). In 1791 Brissot published his book *Nouveau voyage dans les États-Unis de l'Amérique septentrionale* (New Journey in the United States of North America) in three volumes, the book to which Gentz refers. Brissot was one of the most influential writers in the course of the French Revolution. His early works on legislation, his many pamphlets, and his speeches in the Legislative Assembly and the Convention propagate the principles of the French Revolution. Brissot was put to trial by Danton and others and guillotined.

42. William Pitt the Elder, first earl of Chatham (1708–78), twice prime minister of Britain, see above note 15. John Wilkes (1725–97) was an English radical, journalist, and politician.

The Lord Chatham–Wilkes controversy concerned charges of libel against Wilkes and his being ousted from the House of Commons because of the charges.

43. George Washington, the first among the founding fathers, first president of the United States of America. Gentz published an essay on Washington in his *Historisches Journal* (Berlin, 1800), 300–316. In this essay as well, he contends that the American Revolution is completely different from the French Revolution (ibid. 303).

44. Them, that is, the members of the American Congress.

45. Charles Gravier, comte de Vergennes (1717–87), was a French statesman and diplomat. He served as foreign minister from 1774 until his death in 1787 during the reign of Louis XVI, notably during the American War of Indepen-

dence (Great Britain had in the same span of time probably eight times as many foreign ministers—and prime ministers). Vergennes expected that, by giving French aid to the American rebels, he would weaken Britain's dominance of the international stage in the wake of the British victory in the Seven Years' War.

Historians agree today that France's support for the American Revolution produced mixed results and confirm Gentz's assessment of the effect that the French support for the American Revolution had on France. In spite of securing American independence, France was unable to extract considerable material gain from the new U.S. government. Rather the costs of fighting damaged French national finances and furthered the rise of the French Revolution.

46. Gentz refers to the internal devastations of the French Revolution and to the devastations abroad by the wars that the French revolutionary army brought to France's neighboring countries.

47. Gentz acknowledges the influence of the Americans on the French Revolution but considers it to be unintentional on the American side and a perversion of the American ideas through the work of a "hostile Demon" on the French side.

48. The Feuillants as a political group emerged from a split within the Jacobins from those opposing the overthrow of the king and proposing a constitutional monarchy. The deputies publicly split with the Jacobins when they published a pamphlet on July 16, 1791. The group held meetings in a former monastery of the Feuillants on the rue Saint-Honoré, in Paris, and came to be popularly called the *Club des Feuillants*. They called themselves *Amis de la Constitution* (Friends of the Constitution).

49. The Jacobins were the members of the Jacobin Club

(1789–94), who promulgated radical, democratic, and egalitarian ideas. At the time of the French Revolution, the term was often loosely applied to all promulgators of revolutionary positions.

50. Throughout his life and in almost all of his works, Gentz opposed the claim of the French Revolution to have the right to revolutionize all of Europe and of the world. He fought against the missionary aggressiveness of the French Republic during the revolutionary period and its continuation during the Napoleonic era, which brought one wave of warfare after the other to the Continent.

See John Quincy Adams's judgment on the situation of Europe in 1801 after the French Revolution and during the years of Napoleon's consulate in John Quincy Adams, "Letter to Thomas Boylston Adams, dated (Berlin) 14 February, 1801," in *The Writings of John Quincy Adams*, loc. cit., vol. 2, 500–501: "What a number of sovereign states have been swallowed up in the vortex of the last ten years, for the crime of being weak and unable to resist an invading army! What a number more are upon the point of suffering the same fate! The tendency of Europe is so manifestly towards consolidation that, unless it should suddenly and unexpectedly take a different turn, in a few years there will be not more than four or five sovereign states left of the hundreds which covered the surface of this quarter of the globe. An army, therefore, is as necessary to every European power which has any hope of long existence as air to the motion of the lungs, and France through the whole course of the revolution has been so convinced of this, that she has not only kept on foot such armed myriads hitherto, but has settled for her peace establishment one of the largest armies in Europe. Now it is impossible that such armies should be levied, recruited, and maintained, without principles and measures of continual compulsion upon the people. Hence France in her republican state has continued to practice them under the name of conscription, and requisition, and loan, more than the most despotic of enemies."

As to the United States he expects: "A large *permanent* army can never be necessary to us. The only occasion which can require a great military force will be to withstand external invasion, a danger to which we shall become daily less exposed as our population and strength increase." [italics in the original]

51. The French First Republic was never officially proclaimed. On September 21, 1792, the newly established National Convention united for the first time and decided upon the abolition of the monarchy in France. On September 22, 1792, the decision was made to date the acts from the Year I of the Republic, which is often taken as the beginning of the republic. On September 25, 1792, the republic was declared to be "one and indivisible." The First Republic lasted until the declaration of the First French Empire in 1804 under Napoleon.

52. See note 41 on Brissot.

Jean-Paul Marat (1743–93) was a Swiss-born physician, political theorist, and scientist but is better known as a radical journalist and politician from the French Revolution. His journalism was renowned for its uncompromising position toward the new government and "enemies of the revolution" and for basic reforms in favor of the poorest members of society. He enjoyed the trust of the people and was their unofficial link to the Jacobin group that came to power in June 1793. For the two months leading up to the downfall of the Girondin faction in June 1795, he was one of the three most important men in France, alongside Georges Danton and Maximilien Robespierre. He was murdered in his bathtub by Charlotte Corday, a Girondin sympathizer.

Federalists: After the fall of the Girondists in June 1795, the provinces and cities like Marseille, Lyon, and Bordeaux agreed to cut back the power of the revolutionary government in Paris in favor of a more federalist government of France. The debate centered on the question of who represented the sovereignty of the people of France, the people from the provinces or from Paris.

Unitists: The term *unitists* is used here by Gentz as the opposite term to federalists for the centralist fraction of the French Revolution, represented by the revolutionary political clubs in Paris.

Girondists (in French, *Girondins*, or *Brissotins*, after Brissot, who was their most prominent leader, or *Baguettes*): Political fraction in France within the Legislative Assembly and the National Convention during the French Revolution. The Girondists were a group of loosely affiliated individuals rather than an organized political party with a clear ideology. The name was at first informally applied because the most prominent exponents of their point of view were deputies from the Department Gironde ("departments," or *départements,* were regional divisions in France, similar to counties, introduced by the French Revolution to replace the traditional provinces), in Bordeaux. They were less radical than the Jacobins but still followers of the French Revolution.

Mountaineers (*les Montagnards*), or The Mountain (*La Montagne*): Group at the National Convention favoring the republic and opposing the Girondists. The representatives that were the most to the left at the Legislative Assembly of 1791 took the name Mountaineers, because they sat in the highest part of the Assembly, "the mountain"; whereas the representatives of the more-moderate members took the name Plains, or Marshes (*Plaine,* or *Marais*), because they sat on the lower benches of the Assembly.

Dantonians: The followers of Georges Jacques Danton (1759–94). Danton associated with the Mountaineers, on whom he exerted a moderating influence. He also supported the Girondists at times. Gentz uses Danton's example for showing the changing alliances during the French Revolution.

Hebertists (*Hébertistes*): The followers of Jacques René Hébert (1757–94). Hébert was editor of the extreme radical newspaper *Le Père Duchesne*. He himself is sometimes called *Père Duchesne*, after his newspaper. Hébert's atheist movement initiated a religious campaign in order to dechristianize French society.

53. The Reign (or System) of Terror (*la Terreur*) lasted from September 5, 1793, to July 27, 1794. It was a period of violence that occurred after the onset of the French Revolution, caused by conflicts between rival political factions, the Girondins and the Jacobins, and was marked by mass executions of "enemies of the revolution." Estimates vary widely as to how many were killed, with numbers ranging from 16,000 to 40,000. The guillotine ("national razor") became the symbol of a series of executions of such notables as Louis XVI, Marie Antoinette, members of the Girondists, Louis Philippe II, Madame Roland, and Antoine Lavoisier ("the father of modern chemistry"), as well as many others.

54. The Constitution of the Year Three of the French Republic was voted for by the National Convention on August 17, 1795, and was ratified by plebiscite in September 1795. It was effective from September 26 of the same year and handed the supreme power over to the Directory (*Directoire*).

55. Gentz recognizes an increasing degree of warfare after the foundation of the French Republic in 1792 in the French Revolutionary Wars with the culmination in 1795, when the French army attacked the Netherlands and founded the Batavian Republic. After the radical Directory had seized the supreme

power in September 1795, external warfare increased even further in 1796, when the revolutionary army attacked Germany, Austria, and Italy and marched on Vienna and Milan.

56. The French Republic absolved the subjects of the monarchical states of their obedience to their lawful monarchs and their governments on grounds of the revolutionary principles of popular sovereignty and the rights of man.

57. The French Revolution is an assault on the real right of states in the name of abstract and fictional revolutionary principles according to Gentz. If the French Republic absolves the subjects of the European states from their obedience to their lawful governments, it creates a situation like the religious wars, when religious groups claimed to have the divine right to absolve their believers from their duty of obedience as citizens or subjects.

58. Lewis the XIVth, that is, Louis XIV of France, who had started attacking France's neighbors and made large conquests in the Spanish Netherlands and in German lands on the left side of the Rhine, particularly in the Habsburg land of Alsace. But he did not realize his ambition to extend France's eastern border all along the left bank of the Rhine as the French Revolutionary War of 1796 succeeded in doing.

59. Gentz points to the fact that the American Revolution in contrast with the French Revolution did not attack the rights and possessions of private persons. It did not touch property rights and what in the European law tradition would be called civil and private law in contrast to public law. One could object to Gentz's position that the American Revolution did not have to attack the order of property rights, since the transition to a bourgeois society in contrast to an aristocratic society had already been completed in the English revolutions.

60. The French Revolution is in Gentz's view a violent revolt

against the bounds of real right and the nature of things, against valid and positive right as well as the facticity of history.

61. In British politics, the name "Tories" was used for the party of those who were more conservative and supported the rights of the kings, whereas the name "Whigs" was used for the party of those who were more liberal and supported the rights of parliament. In application to the American politics of the time of the American Revolution, the American Tories supported the British crown against the campaign for independence, whereas the American Whigs supported the right of the North American Continental Congresses, as the "parliament" of the colonies, to declare independence from Britain.

62. The term *assignat* was introduced by the French Revolution for bills of credit issued in place of hard currency by the government to cover its costs or debt. In the American Revolution, the same measure was used even earlier to finance the war of independence: bills of credit (paper currency receivable for future taxes). Both revolutions used paper money particularly to cover the costs of war. In both countries, the paper money depreciated quickly. See H. A. Scott Trask, "Inflation and the American Revolution," in *Mises Daily*, July 18, 2003 (online at http://mises.org/story/1273); and William Graham Sumner, *The Financier and the Finances of the American Revolution*, 2 vols., 1891 (reprint New York: Burt Franklin, 1970).

63. For Ramsay see note 36.

Index

Editorial endnotes are indicated by n; thus 96n1 indicates note 1 on page 96. Authorial footnotes are indicated by *; 11*, therefore, indicates the note at the bottom of page 11.

The typeface used for this book is ITC New Baskerville, based on the types of the English type founder and printer John Baskerville (1706–75). Baskerville is the quintessential transitional face: it retains the bracketed and oblique serifs of old-style faces such as Caslon and Garamond, but it presages modern faces in its increased lowercase height, lighter color, and enhanced contrast between thick and thin strokes.

This book is printed on paper that is acid-free and meets the requirements of the American National Standard for Permanence of Paper for Printed Library Materials, z39.48-1992. ⊛

Cover design by Richard Hendel,
Chapel Hill, North Carolina

Typography by Graphic Composition, Inc.,
Bogart, Georgia

Printed and bound by Thomson-Shore,
Dexter, Michigan.